Paul

Shapes

Christianity

Larry W. Wilson

Copyright © 2020

Wake Up America Seminars, Inc.
P.O. Box 273, Bellbrook, Ohio 45305
(800) 475-0876

ISBN 978-0-9668099-9-2

First edition, September 2020
Second printing, July 2021

Paul Shapes Christianity

Table of Contents

Preface

Paul's letters are unusually difficult for Christians to understand. First, they often dealt with topics that have no meaning among Christians today. Today, there is no controversy over food offered to idols or the necessity of circumcision. Second, Christianity then was embryonic, constantly challenged with the pervasive culture, theology, and heritage of Judaism. Paul was faced with the task of persuading Jewish believers in Jesus to let go of Judaism's "salvation by works" orientation to embrace one based on faith through the transforming power of the Holy Spirit. Third, Paul was confronted with the very complicated matter of explaining to Gentile converts the importance of obeying God's laws while also explaining to Jewish converts why Moses' laws were abolished. Fourth, there was a great deal of social friction between Jews and Gentiles, and Paul had the impossible task of convincing new believers to let go of their long-standing bias and hostility toward each other so they could genuinely love one another. Last, when Paul wrote the books of Galatians, Ephesians, Colossians, and Romans, the New Testament did not exist. He was guided by the revelations he directly received from Jesus. Because Paul was well-educated and steeped in Jewish culture, some of his arguments are difficult to understand unless you understand how Jewish traditions were woven into Old Testament cultures and law.

When these five factors are brought together, you can see why there is confusion regarding Paul's writings. When one quotes a verse from Paul and another an opposing verse, the net effect is nonsense. When the Bible is placed in a state of internal conflict, the result is harmful. In my opinion, no writer in the Bible is misquoted more often than Paul. Therefore, it is highly important that Christians study these books as one unit to appreciate his approach to the obstacles previously mentioned. Paul did not speak out of both sides of his mouth. One of his epistles cannot give a fair assessment of what he thought and taught because each one confronts the five obstacles in different ways. However, when the four epistles are studied as one unit, Paul's position and the principles he espoused become quite clear. Personally, I think all fourteen of his letters are wonderful, but my book will be limited to Paul's letters to the Galatians, Ephesians, Colossians, and Romans. In this commentary, my goal is to let Paul do most of the talking. I have inserted and emphasized words enabling you to follow his logic. My words are interlaced in the Bible text and enclosed in brackets [ ]. For best results, have your favorite Bible translation handy as you read.

Larry Wilson

July 2020

Galatians

Introduction

Galatians was written around A.D. 50 – about twenty years after Jesus ascended. Paul wrote this epistle when he became upset with the apostasy of Christians in Galatia. This explains his combative tone and abrasive arguments. "Experts" from Jerusalem were canvassing the territory for followers and, in many cases, successfully challenging, and winning over, Paul's converts to a "better gospel." "These apologists," as I call them, were, no doubt, well-meaning, sincere, and respectable. They desparately wanted and had carefully crafted an argument of a new gospel of unity to end two decades of conflict between Judaism and Christianity. This "better gospel" required Jewish converts to add some Mosaic laws to their practice of Christianity and Paul could not remain silent about the corruption.

The apologists insisted that Christians must observe *some* of the laws of Moses.[1] They reasoned that if Christians obeyed those laws, Israel's leaders would accept Christians as brothers since other sects, like Sadducees and Pharisees, existed within Judaism. When Paul heard this, he became "unglued" and adamantly opposed the apologists.

Paul knew the laws of Moses were temporary. God gave them at Mt. Sinai and they were to remain in effect until Jesus died on the cross. Paul's letters to the Ephesians and Hebrews reveal he had this knowledge. More importantly, Paul knew God did not ordain adding *some* of these laws to Christianity; he knew it to be impossible to obey the Mosaic laws without doing everything they required. The apostate gospel of the apologists was a pretext for adding *all* Mosaic laws later on. If Christianity chose this road, who would have the authority to determine which laws were binding and which were not? Surely, the high priest or Sanhedrin in Jerusalem could not pontificate on this matter, because Christians had a high priest from

---

1   Galatians 4

the tribe of Judah who was in heaven seated at the right hand of God!

Paul was also concerned that new Christians would fall into the same religious trap the Jews had. He knew by experience how religion could squelch the work of the Holy Spirit and end up taking God's place.[1]

After his conversion, Paul could see the wreck that Judaism had made of his life. He was so blinded by loyalty to his religion that he joined in murdering Stephen! At the time, he truly believed he was doing God's will; Deuteronomy 13 gave him permission and authority. When Jesus arrested him on the Damascus road and revealed that God was not pleased with his actions, Paul's mission in life and religious zeal imploded.

Given his experience, Paul was concerned the churches in Galatia would abandon the influence of the Holy Spirit and the gospel of Jesus if they embraced the apologists' lies. He did not want Christianity following in the footsteps of Judaism: a religion of meeting obligations to be righteous in God's sight. This had been his life as a Pharisee. After his conversion, Paul understood the pernicious steps that eventually caused Israel, who professed to love God, to actually hate God when He appeared in the flesh. If the churches in Galatia followed in Israel's steps, the result would be the same.

---

1   See Appendix to Galatians.

Galatians - Part I

Galatians Chapter 1

Galatians 1:1-5: "Paul, an apostle – sent not from men nor by a man, but by Jesus Christ and God the Father, who raised him from the dead – and all the brothers and sisters with me, To the churches in Galatia: Grace and peace to you from God our Father and the Lord Jesus Christ, who gave himself for our sins to rescue us from the present evil age, according to the will of our God and Father, to whom be glory for ever and ever. Amen."

Galatians 1:6-9: "[I am writing to you because] I am astonished that you are so quickly deserting [the gospel I taught you. I am] the one who called you to live in the grace of Christ and [now you] are turning to a different gospel – which is really no gospel at all. Evidently some people are throwing you into confusion and are trying to pervert the gospel of Christ. But even if we or an angel from heaven should preach a gospel other than the one we preached to you, let them be under God's curse [because the gospel I presented to you is based on Scripture and our Lord, Jesus Christ, Himself]! As we have already said, so now I say again: If anybody is preaching to you a gospel other than what you accepted [from me], let them be under God's curse!"

Galatians 1:10-17: "[Because I love you, I must speak boldly and no doubt, some of you will become angry with me.] Am I now trying to win the approval of human beings, or of God? Or am I trying to please people? If I were still trying to please people [as I did when I lived as a Pharisee], I would not be a servant of Christ. I want you to know, brothers and sisters, that the gospel I preached [to you] is not of human origin. I did not receive it from any man, nor was I taught it [in school]; rather, I received it by revelation from Jesus Christ. For you have heard of my previous way of life in Judaism,

how intensely I [hated Christians and zealously] **persecuted the church of God and tried to destroy it. I was advancing in** [the leadership of] **Judaism, beyond many of my own age among my people and was extremely zealous for** [protecting] **the traditions of my fathers. But when God, who set me apart from my mother's womb and called me by his grace, was pleased to reveal his Son in me so that I might preach him among the Gentiles, my immediate response was not to consult any human being. I did not go up to Jerusalem to see those who were apostles before I was, but I went into** [the wilderness of] **Arabia** [to study and learn from the Holy Spirit]. **Later I returned to Damascus."**

Galatians 1:18-24: **"Then after three years** [in the wilderness, carefully studying the Old Testament and aligning Scripture with the visions given me], **I went up to Jerusalem to get acquainted with Cephas [Peter] and stayed with him fifteen days. I saw none of the other apostles – only James, the Lord's brother** [who was the overseer of the church in Jerusalem]. **I assure you before God that what I am writing you is no lie. Then I went to Syria and Cilicia. I was personally unknown to the churches of Judea that are in Christ. They only heard the report: 'The man who formerly persecuted us is now preaching the faith he once tried to destroy.' And** [after they heard my gospel] **they praised God because of me."**

Galatians Chapter 2

Galatians 2:1-3: **"Then** [after my conversion to Christ, I lived and worked among the Gentiles for several years. It was] **after fourteen years, I went up again to Jerusalem, this time with Barnabas. I took Titus along also. I went in response to a revelation** [that was given to me] **and, meeting privately with those esteemed as leaders, I presented to them** [James and the apostles] **the gospel that I preach among the Gentiles. I wanted to be sure I was not running** [contrary to the teachings of the other apostles] **and had not been running my race in vain. Yet not even Titus, who was with me, was compelled** [by James and the apostles] **to be circumcised, even though he was a** [an uncircumcised] **Greek."**

In fact, as a result of Paul's meeting, the group wrote a letter to all Gentiles which stated, *"The apostles and elders, your brothers [at Jerusalem], To the Gentile believers in Antioch, Syria and Cilicia: Greetings. We have heard that some went out from us without our authorization and disturbed you, troubling your minds by what they said [which was, 'You must be circumcised and keep the law of Moses,' but we gave them no such commandment]. So we all agreed to choose some men and send them to you with our dear friends Barnabas and Paul – men who have risked their lives for the name of our Lord Jesus Christ. Therefore we are sending Judas and Silas to confirm by word of mouth what we are writing. It seemed good to the Holy Spirit and to us not to burden you with anything beyond the following requirements: You are to abstain from food sacrificed to idols, from [drinking animal] blood, from [eating] the meat of strangled animals and from sexual immorality. You will do well to avoid these things. Farewell."*[1]

Galatians 2:4-8: "This matter [of circumcision] **arose** [among Gentiles] **because some false believers** [from Jerusalem] **had infiltrated our ranks to spy on the freedom we have in Christ Jesus and to make us slaves** [to the covenant of circumcision[2]]. **We did not give in to them for a moment, so that the truth of the gospel might be preserved for you. As for those** [believers who also came from Jerusalem to see what I was teaching] **who were held in high esteem – whatever they were makes no difference to me; God does not show favoritism – they added nothing to my message. On the contrary, they recognized** [since the Holy Spirit confirmed my ordination and gospel] **that I had been** [chosen and] **entrusted with the task of preaching**

---

1   Acts 15:23-29, insertions and italics mine
2   Genesis 17:12

the [same] **gospel to the uncircumcised** [Gentiles]**, just as Peter had been to the circumcised** [Jews]**. For God, who was at work in Peter as an apostle to the circumcised** [Jews]**, was also at work in me as an apostle to the Gentiles."**

Galatians 2:9-11: "James, Cephas [Peter] **and John, those esteemed as pillars** [in the church]**, gave me and Barnabas the right hand of fellowship when they recognized the** [divine] **grace given to me. They agreed that we should go to the Gentiles, and they to the circumcised** [Jews]**. All they asked was that we should continue to remember the poor, the very thing I had been eager to do all along.** [But a problem started] **When Cephas** [Peter] **came to Antioch, I** [Paul] **opposed him to his face, because he stood condemned** [he was clearly in the wrong. Even Peter, one of the closest to Jesus while He was on Earth and a highly respected Christian leader, failed to live up to the demands of the gospel of Jesus. He needed to be rebuked in public for the cause of Christ and I did so.]**."**

Galatians 2:12: "For before certain men came from James [after the conference in Jerusalem]**, he** [Peter] **used to eat** [and freely socialize] **with the Gentiles. But when they** [this group of spies who pretended to be converts to Christ] **arrived, he** [Peter] **began to draw back and separate himself from the Gentiles because he was afraid of** [ridicule and criticism by] **those who** [advocated and] **belonged to the circumcision group."**

The "circumcision group" was a group of Jewish converts who insisted all Gentile converts must enter into the covenant of circumcision that God gave to Abraham as an *everlasting* covenant.[1] The circumcision group believed only Abraham's heirs could be saved. Therefore, if any man wanted to be an heir of the promises made to Abraham, he had to be circumcised.

Galatians 2:13-14: "The other Jews [locals belonging to the church] **joined him** [Peter] **in his hypocrisy, so that by their hypocrisy even Barnabas was** [soon confused and] **led astray.**

---

1   Genesis 17:13

When I saw that they were not acting in line with the truth of the gospel [of Christ which treats Jew and Gentile alike], **I said to Cephas** [Peter] **in front of them all, 'You are a Jew, yet you live** [outside Jerusalem] **like a Gentile and not like a Jew.** [Here in Galatia you have ignored numerous Jewish laws and traditions such as eating with Gentiles and foods which were set before idols before they were placed on the table.] **How is it, then, that you force Gentiles to follow Jewish customs?'**

Galatians 2:15-16: "**We** [Christians] **who are Jews by birth and not sinful Gentiles know that a person is not justified** [deemed perfect in God's sight] **by the works of the law** [observing the law], **but** [we know that justification comes] **by faith** [alone] **in Jesus Christ. So we, too** [as former Jews], **have put our faith in Christ Jesus that we may be justified by faith in Christ and not by the works of the law, because by the works of the law no one will be** [or can be] **justified.** [It is impossible for a sinner to obey God's law perfectly at all times. Given enough time, each sinner will fail. Therefore, it is impossible for a sinner to stand before God as though he never sinned. Adam's sin reveals it only takes one sin to ruin a life of perfection.]

Galatians 2:17-19: "**But if, in seeking to be justified** [through faith] **in Christ, we Jews** [evidently] **find ourselves also among the sinners** [because faith in Christ does not abolish the royal law[1] which defines sin], **doesn't that mean that Christ promotes sin? Absolutely not!** [Consider my words to Peter:] **If I rebuild what I** [recently] **destroyed, then I really would be a lawbreaker.** [In other words, if I return to circumcision and the laws of Moses, I will soon prove that I cannot be justified. I am unable to live very long without violating God's laws. I cannot be justified in God's sight if I violate a single law! God designed it this way.] **For through the** [condemnation of the] **law I died to the law** [that is, the law revealed I am a sinner and I cannot save myself from the penalty for sin. Therefore, the only way to

---

1   James 2:8

be perfect before God is this: Believe God's Word and obey the voice of the Holy Spirit. This is the essence of living by faith,] **so that I might live for** [honor] **God.**

Galatians 2:20-21: "I have been crucified with Christ [He died for me and each day I crucify my carnal desires so I can serve Him] **and I no longer live** [according to my will, nor to glorify myself with manmade righteousness]**, but Christ lives in me. The life I now live in the body** [is His, I am focused on glorifying Christ through obedience to His commands. I cannot justify myself because I know I am sinful, therefore]**, I live by faith in the Son of God,** [trusting He will justify me when He sees that my heart's desire is to follow Him and obey His Spirit. There is an important difference between being self-directed and Spirit-led. Those who are self-directed are eager to *achieve* justification. Those who are Spirit-led are eager to *receive* justification. Both groups of people recognize the importance of obedience, but the motives are entirely different. I want to love God and my neighbor as the royal law commands because Jesus] **who loved me and** [also] **gave himself for me. I do not set aside the grace of God** [any longer by trying to establish my own righteousness through works]**, for if righteousness could be gained through** [obeying] **the law, Christ died for nothing!"**

Galatians - Part 2

Paul was a Pharisee and son of a Pharisee.[1] He was zealous and educated as a legalist. After his conversion to Christ and several years of unlearning, Paul became a relentless advocate for the principle that "salvation comes through faith in God alone." He had the wounds and scars of persecution to prove that "faith alone" is far more than intellectual assent to an idea. I think Paul would summarize his *faith alone* position by saying: "First, faith in God means believing God *will do* things for people beyond human ability. Second, faith in God means believing God *will keep* His promises. Third, faith in God means *pleasing* God (fulfilling His laws) without regard for the consequences." When we combine these three concepts, salvation becomes a matter of love and faith. Obeying God's laws cannot produce the righteousness needed for salvation, and this revelation destroyed Paul's zeal for Judaism. Jesus alone produces the righteousness needed for salvation. He overcame every temptation and His righteousness is *transferred* to those who love Him and live by faith. The walk of faith requires us to depend on God who enables us to do things beyond our abilities. This completes the three step loop.

Faith in God is only tested when there is a price to pay for obedience. If a person lives in a setting where obeying God is perpetually comfortable, be suspicious. We live in a dark world where the currents of sin are very strong and constant temptation abounds. God's laws are contrary to the ways of sinners. Temporal comfort can be an enemy to faith. Jesus made this point painfully clear in his rebuke to the believers in Laodicea whom he called lukewarm, blind, and naked.[2] Each disciple of Jesus is given a *mission* so far beyond human ability that many would quit if they could see what the journey involves. Christians today, unfortunately, do not have the faith of Noah, Abraham, Moses, Caleb, or Joshua.

Faith is tested when there is a trial or challenge of some kind, and

---

1   Acts 23:6
2   Revelation 3:14-22

the challenge for the Jewish converts to Christ in Galatia was largely centered on whether centuries of Jewish customs should be abandoned. The social and theological consequences were significant.

Galatians Chapter 3

Galatians 3:1-5: "You foolish Galatians! Who has bewitched you [with religious bamboozle that demands circumcision]? **Before your very eyes Jesus Christ was clearly portrayed as crucified** [for your sins]. **I would like to learn just one thing from you: Did you receive the** [power and the manifestations of the Holy] **Spirit by the works of the law, or by believing what you heard? Are you so foolish** [that you cannot see what you are doing]? **After beginning** [your walk] **by means of the Spirit, are you now trying to finish** [your goal of justification] **by means of the flesh? Have you experienced so much** [ridicule and persecution] **in vain – if it really was in vain? So again I ask, does God give you his Spirit and work miracles among you by the works of the law, or by your believing what you heard?**"

Galatians 3:6-8: "[Let us go back to the origin of circumcision for a moment.] **So also Abraham 'believed God** [when God said he would become the father of many nations even though he had no children], **and** [Genesis says[1]] **it was credited to him as righteousness** [because he did not doubt that God would fulfill His promise].' **Understand, then, that those who have faith** [in God, those who fully rely on God's promises,] **are children of Abraham** [because they believe God's promises just as Abraham believed God's promises[2]]. [Old Testament] **Scripture foresaw** [centuries ago] **that God would** [also] **justify the Gentiles by faith, and** [God] **announced** [this wonderful development in the] **the gospel** [given] **in advance to Abraham** [when He said]: **'All nations** [on Earth] **will be blessed through you.'**"[3]

Galatians 3:9-11: "So those who [live in all of the nations of

1   Genesis 15:6
2   John 8:39
3   This matter is discussed at length in Ephesians.

the world and] **rely on faith** [in God] **are blessed along with Abraham, the man of faith. For all who rely on the works of the law** [to be justified] **are under a curse, as it is written: 'Cursed is everyone who does not continue to do** *everything* **written in the Book of the Law.'**[1] **Clearly no one who relies on the law is justified** [or can be justified] **before God** [by obeying the law]**, because** [the Scriptures say in Habakkuk[2]] **'the righteous will live by faith.'** [This is a critical point: No one but Jesus has lived a sinless life, not even Abraham. Abraham was not justified through obedience. Abraham was not perfect. He lied about his wife Sarah several times because of fear, and committed adultery with Hagar! At times, Abraham let go of his faith in God's promises. He was a sinner, but he was justified by his faith in God! When God called him to leave home and travel to a foreign land, he obeyed!]"

Galatians 3:12: "The law is not based on faith [God's laws are divine obligations which He has imposed on mankind for our benefit]**; on the contrary, it says** [God has said, in Ezekiel[3]]**, 'The person who does these things will live by them.'"**

This declaration means the man who obeys God's laws will thrive and be blessed by them because they are not harmful. They are the product of divine wisdom and bring good results into our lives. Do not be confused, the blessings that come with obeying God's laws and the righteousness needed for salvation are two separate issues. For example, the law says 'Thou shalt not steal.' If I do not steal his possessions, my neighbor is blessed and so am I. My neighbor suffers no loss and I am not condemned as a thief. However, if I do not steal my neighbor's possessions, I have not necessarily fulfilled the intent of God's law. The royal law is fulfilled when I love my neighbor enough that I would rather cut off my hand than to steal his property. Such love is only acquired through faith

---

1   Deuteronomy 27:26
2   Habakkuk 2:4
3   Ezekiel 20:11

in Christ. God has promised to remove our selfishness and unrighteousness and give us a new heart.[1] If I am tempted to steal (which is a selfish desire), perhaps I can be victorious over this temptation a few times through willpower, but this is not the way of Christ! Jesus has made two promises: First, He has promised to transform us from within by sending the Holy Spirit to create a clean heart and renew a right spirit within us if we ask Him. This process is called rebirth.[2] Second, He will give us victory over temptation by displacing selfish passions with love and divine power.[3] If we ask for transformation and believe it will come, He will send it! He has also promised to put a new heart in every person who asks for it.

The purpose of God's law is to function as a mirror. It shows our weaknesses, our deviation from righteousness, and our desperate need for a Savior. God's laws are not opposed to the ministry of the Spirit. Instead, our sinful nature is opposed to God's laws.[4] The Ten Commandments are called a covenant because they are a promise. God promises that when we love Him with all of our heart, mind, and soul, and our neighbor as ourselves, we will fulfill the law by living in perfect harmony with His law. For a sinner, the law is indispensable since it declares right from wrong; it represents a righteousness that a sinner cannot produce. The good news is that Jesus fulfilled the law, He has promised to give His righteousness to all repentant sinners, and He will send transforming power to everyone who seeks it.[5] Do you believe His promises?

Galatians 3:13-15: "Christ redeemed us [believers] **from the curse of the law** [which is eternal death] **by becoming a curse for us, for it is written: 'Cursed is everyone who is hung on a pole.'**[6] [The Father] **He redeemed us** [through Jesus' death] **in order that**

---

1   1 John 1:9; Ezekiel 36:26
2   Ezekiel 36:26; John 3
3   Romans 6:14-23; 8:14
4   Romans 8:5-8
5   Romans 1:16-17; Acts 1:8
6   Deuteronomy 21:23

the [promised] **blessing given to Abraham might** [also] **come to the Gentiles through Christ Jesus, so that by faith we** [Jews and Gentiles alike] **might receive the promise of the** [Holy] **Spirit** [who transforms our rebellious minds and sanctifies our sinful hearts. The Spirit enables us to love God and our neighbors wholeheartedly because this is humanly impossible]. **Brothers and sisters, let me take an example from everyday life. Just as no one can set aside or add to a human covenant that has been duly established, so it is in this case."**

Galatians 3:16-18: "[God gave three promises to Abraham. First, God promised his descendants would be given possession of the land. Second, God promised Abraham he would become the father of many nations. Third, God promised Abraham that through him, the nations of Earth would be blessed–meaning the Savior of *the whole world* would come through his bloodline.] **The** [three] **promises were spoken to Abraham and to his seed** [notice the singular]. [If you examine the promises in Genesis,[1]] **Scripture does not say 'and to seeds,'** [plural] **meaning many people, but** [the promise says] **'and to your seed,' meaning one person, who is Christ. What I mean is this: The law** [given at Mt. Sinai], [was] **introduced 430 years later** [after the three promises were given to Abraham. The law given at Mt. Sinai]**, does not set aside the covenant previously established by God and thus do away with the promise[s]. For if the inheritance depends on** [observing] **the law, then it no longer depends on the promise; but God in his grace gave it to Abraham through a promise."**

Galatians 3:19-20: "[I know this letter will be challenged by false brothers who have come in among you. They will scoff and ask] **Why, then, was the law given at all** [if salvation depends on faith]? [The answer is obvious.] **It** [the law] **was added because of** [man's darkness and ignorance. God chose to enlighten mankind by giving us His wise and enduring laws to bless us so we can understand the curse, nature, and behavior of sin and

---

1   Genesis 13:15-16; 15:5, 13, 18

the penalty for our] **transgressions until the Seed to whom the promise referred had come.** [We know that any violation of God's laws, whether willful or through ignorance, always brings sorrow, pain, and death, therefore] **The law was given through** [the ministry of] **angels**[1] [who were directed by a mediator] **and** [it was] **entrusted to a mediator** [who represents us before the Father]. **A mediator, however, implies more than one party;** [our mediator understands the needs of fallen man as well as the objectives of the Father] **but** [the] **God** [head] **is one** [in purpose, plan, and action]."

Galatians 3:21-22: "**Is the law** [given at Mt. Sinai]**, therefore, opposed to the** [three] **promises of God** [given to Abraham]? **Absolutely not! For if a law had been given that could impart** [eternal] **life, then righteousness would certainly have come by** [obeying] **the law. But Scripture has locked up everything under the control of sin,** [we have all sinned, we are condemned by our sins and given our sinful nature, no one can live very long without sinning] **so** [God has provided a better way for us to receive] **that what was promised** [to Abraham]**,** [the promise] **being given** [has been extended to all mankind, Jew and Gentile alike] **through faith in Jesus Christ,** [who are Abraham's seed, so that everything] **might be given to those who believe** [in God as Abraham believed in God]."

Galatians 3:23-24: "**Before the coming** [arrival] **of this faith** [before Jesus came to Earth]**, we** [Jews] **were held in custody under the law,** [we were] **locked up** [and confused in matters of grace, faith, and obedience] **until the faith** [in God] **that was to come would be revealed** [that is, properly demonstrated and clarified by the life and teachings of Jesus]**. So the law was our guardian** [at Mt. Sinai to show us our sinful nature and propensity for sin] **until** [it should have led us to understand our need for a Savior who could save us sinners from our sins. For fourteen centuries Israel conducted sacrifices on the Altar of

---

1   Exodus 23:20-23; 32:34; 33:2

Burnt Offering and very few understood our great need for the Lamb of God. We foolishly thought we were righteous because we did what God commanded. Little did we know that the blood of animals could not take away our sins![1] Our foolishness changed when] **Christ came** [to Earth and now we see there is a difference between obeying the law and obeying the Spirit so] **that we might be justified by faith** [alone]."

Galatians 3:25: **"Now that this faith** [has been demonstrated and clarified through Christ who] **has come** [into the world], **we are no longer under a guardian** [the supervision of the law to understand the curse of sin, the sinful nature, and our desperate need of a Savior]. [Jesus has explained the relationship between grace, faith, and law. According to the Father's grace, the promises given to Abraham include all repentant sinners, Jews and Gentiles alike. The fulfillment of the promises has been made possible through the perfect life of Jesus.]"

Galatians 3:26-29: **"**[In summary, if you will follow Jesus and live by faith, then] **So in Christ Jesus you are all children of God through faith, for all of you who were baptized into Christ have clothed yourselves with Christ**['s righteousness]. **There is neither Jew nor Gentile, neither slave nor free, nor is there male and female, for you are all one in Christ Jesus.** [Therefore, the covenant of physical circumcision ended at the cross. No longer does God consider a man an heir of Abraham because of physical circumcision. Moses said the circumcision that matters to God is the circumcision of the heart.[2] The flesh of the sinful heart has to be removed so a new heart, transformed by the Spirit, may function. Because] **If you belong to Christ, then you are Abraham's seed** [sperm]**, and heirs according to the** [three] **promise**[s that await fulfillment]."

---

1   Hebrews 10:4
2   Deuteronomy 10:16; 30:6

Galatians - Part 3
Galatians Chapter 4

Galatians 4:1-7: "[I have a few words for my brothers in Christ who are former Jews. Compare the promises given to Abraham with a civil process that you well know.] **What I am saying is that as long as an heir is underage, he is no different from a slave, although he owns the whole estate. The heir is subject to guardians and trustees until the time set by his father. So also, when we** [Jews] **were** [delivered from Egypt, we were spiritually ignorant and rebellious like] **underage** [children], **we were in slavery under the elemental spiritual forces of the world** [that is, we lived as the world does]. **But when the set time had fully come, God sent his Son, born of a woman, born under the** [obligation of His] **law[s], to redeem those under the** [obligation of His] **law[s], that we might receive adoption to sonship.** ['And who,' you may ask, 'is a son of God?' 'Those who are led by the Spirit of God are sons of God.'[1]] **Because you** [have received Jesus as your Savior, you] **are his sons, God sent the** [Holy] **Spirit** [to you, the Holy Spirit serves under the authority] **of his Son** [and He has been sent] **into our hearts, the Spirit who** [reveals the goodness and love of the Father, also] **calls out, '*Abba,*** [a term of endearment meaning, God is also my dear] **Father.' So you** [dear brothers in Christ] **are no longer a slave** [subject to guardians and trustees], **but** [you are] **God's child; and since you are his child, God has made you also an heir.**"

Galatians 4:8-12: "[I have a few words for my brothers in Christ who are former Gentiles.] **Formerly, when you did not know God, you were slaves to those** [idols] **who by nature are not gods** [at all]. [There was a time when you believed it was necessary to appease those gods for fear you would suffer great harm if you did not.] **But now that you know** [the truth about the living] **God – or rather are** [now] **known by God** [as His sons] **– how is it that you are turning back to those weak and miserable**

forces [of living as a slave to some god]? **Do you wish to be enslaved by them all over again?** [Look at your foolishness!] **You** [have embraced the teachings of the false brothers from Jerusalem and you] **are observing special days** [feast days] **and** [you are observing the arrival of new] **months** [with new moon feasts. These religious traditions have nothing to do with serving Christ.] **and** [you are observing the growing] **seasons** [with the presentation of first fruits and the wave sheaf offering] **and** [even attempting to observe Sabbath] **years! I fear for you, that somehow I have wasted my efforts on you. I plead with you, brothers and sisters, become** [free of these matters] **like me, for I became like you. You did me no wrong."**

Galatians 4:13-16: "[I have been told that some in the church have had a change of heart toward me. I am no longer welcome in Galatia.] **As you know, it was because of an illness that I first preached the gospel to you, and even though my illness was a trial to you** [you were very supportive of my physical needs during my recovery], **you did not treat me with contempt or scorn. Instead, you welcomed me as if I were an angel of God, as if I were Christ Jesus himself. Where, then, is your blessing of me now? I can testify that, if you could have done so, you would have torn out your eyes and given them to me. Have I now become your enemy by telling you the truth?"**

Galatians 4:17-20: "**Those people** [from Jerusalem belonging to the circumcision group] **are zealous to win you over** [to a fake gospel of salvation through obedience], **but** [it is] **for no good. What they** [really] **want is to alienate you from us** [who know the wonderful freedom in Christ], **so that you may have zeal for them. It is fine to be zealous, provided the purpose is good, and to be so always, not just when I am with you. My dear children, for whom I am again in the pains of childbirth until** [the ways and joy of] **Christ is formed in you, how I wish I could be with you now and change my tone, because I am perplexed about you!"**

Galatians 4:21-26: "Tell me, you who want to be under the law [you who want to be justified through obedience], **are you not aware of what the law** [the books of Moses] **says? For it is written that Abraham had two sons, one by the slave woman** [Hagar] **and the other by the free woman** [Sarah]. **His son by the slave woman was born according to the flesh** [in the ordinary way], **but his son by the free woman was born as the result of a divine promise** [from God because Sarah was too old to conceive]. **These things are being taken figuratively: The [two] women represent two covenants. One covenant is from Mount Sinai and bears** [produces] **children who are to be slaves** [to the law]: **This is Hagar. Now Hagar stands for Mount Sinai in Arabia** [where the law was given] **and corresponds to the present city of Jerusalem, because she** [Jerusalem] **is in slavery with her children** [the Jews]. [The children of Hagar think they can be saved through obedience and they are slaves to the idea that salvation comes through works of the flesh. I know all about this, for this was my zeal and religion at one time!] **But the [New] Jerusalem that is above is** [comprised of those who believe God's promises even though we cannot enter the city just yet. We are truly] **free, and she** [whom Sarah represents] **is our mother."**

Galatians 4:27-30: "For it is written [in an oracle in Isaiah[1]]: **'Be glad, barren woman** [Sarah], **you who never bore a child; shout for joy and cry aloud, you who were never in labor; because more are the children of the desolate woman** [Sarah] **than of her who has a husband.'** [This oracle caricatures Sarah, who was a barren woman for most of her life. But God kept His promise and she miraculously conceived. The idea is that Sarah – the barren woman – would have many times more children through faith than any woman could have through the works of the flesh.] **Now you,** [Gentile and Jewish] **brothers and sisters** [in the Lord are], **like Isaac,** [you] **are children of promise. At that time the son born according to the flesh**

---

1   Isaiah 54:1

[Ishmael] **persecuted the son** [Isaac] **born by the power of the Spirit. It is the same now. But what does Scripture say?** '[God commanded Abraham] **Get rid of the slave woman and her son, for the slave woman's son will never share in the inheritance with the free woman's son.'"**[1]

Galatians 4:31: "Therefore, brothers and sisters, we [who are believers in Jesus] **are not children of the slave woman** [our righteousness does not come from our obedience], **but** [we are] **of the free woman** [our righteousness comes through Jesus by faith]."

Although obedience is required, a sinner cannot justify himself through obedience because his disobedience always ruins the process. We are truly free from slavery even though the law imposes its obligations upon us. Our joy is in knowing that Christ is our Savior; He is our righteousness. Born-again people want their naturally selfish hearts of flesh transformed (circumcised) each day so we can please Jesus by fulfilling the law, for He justifies everyone who lives by faith. *"For in the gospel the righteousness of God is revealed – a righteousness that is by faith from first to last, just as it is written: 'The righteous will live by faith.'"*[2]

Galatians Chapter 5

Galatians 5:1-2: "It is for freedom that Christ has set us free. Stand firm, then, and do not let yourselves be burdened again by a yoke of slavery. Mark my words! I, Paul, tell you that if you let yourselves be circumcised, Christ will [soon] **be of no value to you at all.** [If you listen to the men from Jerusalem and submit to circumcision, you will slip progressively deeper into the slavery that legalism demands. Your religious experience will be reduced to do's and don'ts (the life of a slave) and the joy of knowing the riches of Christ will fade away. Your religious experience will become a ritual. Your growth in Christ will become stale because there is no faith. Is this what you want?

---

1   Genesis 21:8-13
2   Romans 1:17, italics mine

Do you want to deceive yourselves and think you can save yourselves from eternal death by obedience or do you want to trust God's promises and walk with Him in Spirit and in Truth? Salvation comes to everyone who believes the promises of God. *"For we maintain that a person is justified by faith apart from the works of the law."*[1]]"

Galatians 5:3-6: "Again I declare to every man who lets himself be circumcised that he is obligated to obey the whole law. [You will be obligated to obey more laws than you can count!] **You who are trying to be justified by** [obeying] **the law have been alienated from Christ; you have fallen away from grace** [God's favor]. [Your efforts and Christ's sacrifice have no value.] **For through the Spirit we** [believers] **eagerly await by faith the righteousness for which we hope. For in Christ Jesus neither circumcision nor uncircumcision has any value. The only thing that counts is faith expressing itself through love."**

Galatians 5:7-10: "[My dear children,] **You were running a good race. Who cut in on you** [pun intended] **to keep you from obeying the truth?** [I know who. I am well acquainted with the circumcision group. They love their religious slavery and self-righteousness. I once lived as they live. They foolishly think that rigorous obedience makes a man righteous in God's sight.] **That kind of persuasion does not come from the one** [Holy Spirit] **who calls you** [to follow Christ]. [Jesus said,] **'A little yeast works through the whole batch of dough.'** [This means a little heresy contaminates the whole religion.] **I am confident in the Lord that you will take no other view** [than believing in God's promises]. **The one who is throwing you into confusion, whoever that may be, will have to pay the penalty."**

Galatians 5:11: "Brothers and sisters, if I am still preaching circumcision [as some from Jerusalem falsely claim]**, why am I still being persecuted** [by the Jews]**?** [If I am advocating Judaism, why do they hate me?] **In that case the offense of the**

1   Romans 3:28, italics mine

cross has been abolished. [For the Jews do not accept this truth: Jesus terminated the "everlasting covenant" of circumcision given to Abraham – which was a covenant in the flesh. The Lord has shown me that *"A person is not a Jew who is one only outwardly, nor is circumcision merely outward and physical. No, a person is a Jew who is one inwardly; and circumcision is circumcision of the heart, by the Spirit, not by the written code. Such a person's praise is not from other people, but from God."*[1]]"

Galatians 5:12-15: **"As for those agitators, I wish they would go the whole way and emasculate themselves!** [If they did this, they would have no more offspring! But] **You, my brothers and sisters, were called to be free** [in Christ]. **But** [be careful,] **do not use your freedom to indulge the flesh** [the sinful nature which is naturally hostile toward the laws of God]; **rather,** [humbly accept God's justification through the atonement and righteousness provided by Christ and] **serve one another humbly in love. For the entire law** [pertaining to man's duty to man] **is fulfilled in keeping this one command: 'Love your neighbor as yourself.' If you bite and devour each other, watch out or you will be destroyed by each other."**

Galatians 5:16-17: **"So I say, walk by the Spirit, and you will not gratify the desires of the flesh.** [*"Those who live according to the flesh have their minds set on what the flesh desires; but those who live in accordance with the Spirit have their minds set on what the Spirit desires. The mind governed by the flesh is death, but the mind governed by the Spirit is life and peace. The mind governed by the flesh is hostile to God; it does not submit to God's law, nor can it do so. Those who are in the realm of the flesh cannot please God."*[2]] **For the flesh desires what is contrary to the Spirit, and the Spirit what is contrary to the flesh.** [Be on your guard,] **They** [the flesh and the Spirit] **are in conflict with each other, so that you are not to do whatever you want."**

---

1   Romans 2:28-29, italics mine
2   Romans 8:5-8

Galatians 5:18-24: "**But if you are led by the Spirit, you are not under the law** [as a means for justification]. [Notice how rebellion against God's law works:] **The acts of the flesh are obvious: sexual immorality, impurity and debauchery; idolatry and witchcraft; hatred, discord, jealousy, fits of rage, selfish ambition, dissensions, factions and envy; drunkenness, orgies, and the like. I warn you, as I did before, that those who live like this will not inherit the kingdom of God.** [This is an essential truth. Do not be deceived. You cannot claim to be led by the Spirit and rebel against the laws of God! The Holy Spirit's objective is to draw us into God's presence by putting God's laws in our hearts and minds. How else can we enjoy eternity with God?] **But the fruit of the Spirit is love, joy, peace, forbearance, kindness, goodness, faithfulness, gentleness and self-control. Against such things there is no law. Those who belong to Christ Jesus have crucified the flesh with its passions and** [rebellious and immoral] **desires.**"

Galatians 5:25-26: "**Since we live by the Spirit, let us keep in step with the Spirit** [who knows our thoughts and mind]. **Let us not become conceited, provoking and envying each other.**"

Galatians Chapter 6

Galatians 6:1-5: "**Brothers and sisters, if someone is caught in a sin, you who live by the Spirit should restore that person gently. But watch yourselves, or you also may be tempted. Carry each other's burdens** [concern yourselves with the suffering and temptations of those around you], **and in this way you will fulfill the law of Christ. If anyone thinks they are something** [righteous] **when** [actually,] **they are not, they deceive themselves. Each one should test their own actions** [by looking into the fulfillment of the law and after identifying his or her own failures and successes through faith]. **Then they can take pride in themselves alone, without comparing themselves to someone else, for**

each one should carry their own load [of responsibilities as far as possible]."

Galatians 6:6-10: "Nevertheless, the one who receives instruction in the word should share all good things with their instructor. [Be charitable to those who teach the word and carry its burden.] **Do not be deceived: God cannot be mocked. A man reaps what he sows. Whoever sows to please their flesh, from the flesh will reap destruction; whoever sows to please the Spirit, from the Spirit will reap eternal life. Let us not become weary in doing good, for at the proper time we will reap a** [good] **harvest if we do not give up. Therefore, as we have opportunity, let us do good to all people, especially to those who belong to the family of believers."**

Galatians 6:11-12: "See what large letters I use as I write to you with my own hand! [Because I am nearly blind and no one around me can take dictation, I have written this letter with my own hand.] **Those who want to impress people by means of the flesh are trying to compel you to be circumcised. The only reason they do this is to avoid being persecuted for the cross of Christ.** [They foolishly think the Jews will approve of us if we consent to circumcision. This is totally false. Any compromise or dilution on the importance of the perfect life and sacrificial death of Jesus on the cross will derail the gospel of Christ and in time, Christianity will become absorbed with confusion and darkness just like Judaism.]"

Galatians 6:13-18: "Not even those who are circumcised keep the law, yet they want you to be circumcised that they may boast about your circumcision in the flesh. [They want to return to Jerusalem and say to the high priest, "Look, here are the 'backsliders' who returned to Judaism!"] **May I never boast except in the cross of our Lord Jesus Christ, through which the world has been crucified to me, and I to the world. Neither circumcision nor uncircumcision means anything** [now]; **what counts** [in God's sight] **is the new creation.** [Believe God's promises, love Him and your neighbor, walk by faith, allow the law to serve its purpose and the Holy Spirit will make you a new creation! When God's laws are written in our hearts and minds, His image is restored in us!] **Peace and mercy to all who follow this rule** ["Stop thinking that obedience will bring salvation." I say this] **– to the Israel of God** [who has been separated from ancient Israel.[1]]. **From now on, let no one cause me trouble** [dispute the things which the Lord has revealed to me]**, for I** [am a servant of the Lord Jesus and I] **bear on my body the marks** [and stripes] **of Jesus. The grace of our Lord Jesus Christ be with your spirit, brothers and sisters. Amen."**

---

1   James 1:1; 2:1

Appendix to Galatians

Three Laboratories

According to Hebrews 11, faith has been the key to salvation from the beginning of sin. "By faith Abel. . ." "By faith Enoch . . ." "By faith Noah . . ." This fact is important because there never has been a dispensation where salvation came through works (man's efforts).

Over the past 6,000 years, God has established three laboratories for the universe to study. Each laboratory is different, but the key to salvation is the same. The first laboratory existed from the fall of Adam and Eve until Noah's flood. During this time, the gospel was passed down from father to son. The Ten Commandments were made known through divine revelation but not written. Laws regarding animal sacrifices were also known and followed at certain intervals of time but these laws were not written either. These select few obligations were imposed on mankind during this laboratory. However, after sixteen centuries, God had to destroy the whole world because of violence and wickedness.

Then came the laboratory which existed from Mt. Sinai until Jesus' death. During this period, God delivered a nation of slaves from Egypt, spoke the Ten Commandments to them, and dictated many laws to Moses. God's will for His people has never been more clearly stated than at Mt. Sinai. However, Israel's history proves that, corporately speaking, sinners are unable to carry out God's will, even when there is no dispute over it! After fourteen centuries of patient endurance, God destroyed Israel in A.D. 70.

The third laboratory began on the day of Pentecost in Acts 2 and it will last until the 144,000 are selected and sealed. During this time period, God has used the failures of the two previous laboratories to inform and educate sinners about His ways. Additionally, He gave us the apostles and many gifts through the ministry of the Holy Spirit.

However, after twenty centuries of patient endurance, Christianity has failed. Today it mirrors Israel's apostasy. This is why God will soon raise up 144,000 people to accomplish the gospel commission.

Remember, Paul as a former Pharisee, understood that a highly structured religion can squelch the work of the Holy Spirit and worse, it can end up taking God's place. This is why Paul insists on following the Spirit! If the Holy Spirit convicts a person he should do something, he must do it, even if it involves leaving home as Abraham did. Of course, Paul clearly teaches that the Holy Spirit would never convict a person to do something that is outside God's will.

Now that two thousand years have passed, we see the awful result of this laboratory. Corporately speaking, Christianity has followed the spirit of man instead of the Spirit of God. Sinners justify themselves by separating themselves from God's Word. For the sinner, tradition is more important than truth. Therefore, faith is not defined through obedience to the Holy Spirit; it is instead whatever a person wishes to believe!

If Paul were resurrected today, he would become angry seeing the condition of Christianity. He would be more abrasive and combative with Christians today than with the Christians in Galatia. Paul would confront the notion that God's amazing grace is a license for lawlessness, and would call out the vanity that permeates Christianity. As Jesus said, **"These people honor me with their lips, but their hearts are far from me. They worship me in vain; their teachings are merely human rules."**[1]

When we examine these three laboratories, what does God want us to see? First, He wants us to see that sinners will always fail to live up to the righteousness needed for salvation. Second, He wants us to see that the leading of the Holy Spirit is always contrary to the sinful nature. **"And if the Spirit of him who raised Jesus from the dead is living in you, he who raised Christ from the dead will also give life to your mortal bodies because of his Spirit who lives in you.**

---

1   Matthew 15:8-9

Therefore, brothers and sisters, we have an obligation—but it is not to the flesh, to live according to it. For if you live according to the flesh, you will die; but if by the Spirit you put to death the misdeeds of the body, you will live. For those who are led by the Spirit of God are the children of God."[1]

The Church Bipolar

Jewish converts came into the early Christian church with a strong dislike for Gentiles who were considered unclean (Acts 10), and a mindset heavily influenced by centuries of legalism that affected every aspect of life,[2] Gentile converts came into the church with feelings of anti-Semitism, a culture of pagan practices, and resistance for obeying any rules that militated against the desires of the flesh.[3] Jewish converts were inclined to carry on with the laws of Moses. Gentiles wanted a salvation that had nothing to do with sanctification. *It is the presence of these two extremes within the body of Christ that makes the writings of Paul difficult to understand.* Today, these two extremes still exist within the body of Christ and each group uses the writings of Paul to defend its theology.

Obeying the Law is Not Necessarily Fulfilling the Law

There is a significant difference between obeying and fulfilling the Ten Commandments. Any discussion about any commandment should address this difference. The two *laws of love*[4] are expressed in the Ten Commandments. The first four commandments declare what love for God will do and the remaining six commandments declare what love for our neighbor will do. Paul wrote, **"The commandments, 'You shall not commit adultery,' 'You shall not murder,' 'You shall not steal,' 'You shall not covet,' and whatever other command there may be, are summed up in this one command: 'Love your neighbor as yourself.' Love does no harm to a neighbor. Therefore love is the fulfillment of the law."[5]**

---

1   Romans 8:11-14
2   Acts 15:5
3   Galatians 5:15-21
4   Matthew 22:36-40
5   Romans 13:9-10

What did Jesus say about love for God? **"If you love me, keep my commands."**[1] **"You are my friends if you do what I command."**[2]

Everyone in the universe is subject to God's laws. Jesus immediately put Adam and Eve under the obligation of law when He created them. **"And the Lord God commanded the man, 'You are free to eat from any tree in the garden; but you must not eat from the tree of the knowledge of good and evil, for when you eat from it you will certainly die.'"**[3] Adam and Eve could not have sinned if there was no law because where there is no law there is no sin.[4] Sin, by definition, is lawlessness – a disregard for God's laws.[5] The Ten Commandments are not suggestions. They are divine laws written in stone and Jesus commands everyone obey them, but not to achieve salvation.

God designed the Ten Commandments with two purposes for human beings: First, on a secular level, the Ten Commandments were to produce social order. If everyone obeyed the Ten Commandments, there would be goodwill within and among the families that make up every nation. There would be no valid reason for hatred or animus. Nations prosper when a majority obeys and exalts the divine principles expressed in the Ten Commandments.

The Ten Commandments were also designed to serve a second and higher purpose. Once a person is born again, he discovers the Ten Commandments predict the actions of a pure heart: what an honest-hearted person will do when he loves God and man properly. In other words, the law of the kingdom of God (royal law) reveals what pure-hearted beings will naturally do! **"The law of the Lord is perfect, refreshing the soul. The statutes of the Lord are trustworthy, making wise the simple. The precepts of the Lord are right, giving joy to the heart. The commands of the Lord are radiant, giving light to the eyes. The fear of the Lord is pure, enduring forever. The decrees of the Lord are firm, and all of**

---

1   John 14:15
2   John 15:14
3   Genesis 2:16-17
4   Romans 4:15
5   1 John 3:4

them are righteous. They are more precious than gold, than much pure gold; they are sweeter than honey, than honey from the honeycomb."[1]

Consider the operation of God's law: If a secular man obeys the seventh commandment which forbids adultery because the law demands it, his family, his children, and even his coworkers will be blessed. There's no scandal or bitterness caused by unfaithfulness. There is social peace and harmony. Later, suppose this man's lust overcomes him and he violates the seventh commandment. The social benefit of the seventh commandment is lost. His wife and children are betrayed and made bitter. His wife is broken and sues for divorce. His coworkers are upset because he cannot do his job. There is assuredly a secular benefit for obeying the seventh commandment as well as the other nine.

"But each person is tempted when they are dragged away by their own evil desire and enticed. Then, after desire has conceived, it gives birth to sin; and sin, when it is full-grown, gives birth to death. Don't be deceived, [sinful desires can pop up at any time, so be on your guard] **my dear brothers and sisters."**[2]

Now, consider a second scenario that contrasts the temporal and spiritual purpose for the seventh commandment. One day, a married but born-again man is tempted to have a sexual relationship with an attractive woman, and given human nature and the rush of hormones, he faces a powerful temptation. Immediately, the Holy Spirit pounds on his heart with this impression: "Flee! You must not do this. If you sin, you will prove that you don't love God or your wife as you should!" At this point the man should ask himself if he has been fulfilling the seventh commandment or merely observing the seventh commandment! Suppose he has lived within the boundaries of the seventh commandment for many years, should he be alarmed that he finds another woman tempting?

---

1   Psalm 19:7-10
2   James 1:14-16, insertion mine

Consider this: Jesus said, **"You have heard that it was said, 'You shall not commit adultery.' But I tell you that anyone who looks at a woman lustfully has already committed adultery with her in his heart."**[1] Contrary to what is often said about this passage, Jesus spoke these words to highlight the fact that a great gulf exists between *observing* the seventh commandment and *fulfilling its intent*. If the man in this scenario has observed the seventh commandment because it is God's law, there is some temporal benefit; there is no scandal and his family remains intact. However, it is possible the man missed the higher and more important reason for the seventh commandment.

God knows all about the curse of sin. He knows we are attracted to evil and, worse, we have a propensity for evil. To counteract the curse and our propensity, He has promised if we will love Him with all of our heart, mind, and soul, and our neighbors as ourselves, He will miraculously transform us. He will write His laws in our hearts and minds, and as children of God, we will reflect His character of love. This is why the Ten Commandments are called a covenant. They are God's promise![2]

The Ten Commandments have temporal and spiritual value. The man who rests on the Sabbath because the law requires it, receives the temporal benefit of rest. The man who rests on the Sabbath so that He can have communion with His Creator is blessed more! Its higher value is the spiritual value.[3] The spiritual component of the Ten Commandments explains a mystery. James wrote: **"For whoever keeps the whole law and yet stumbles at just one point is guilty of breaking all of it."**[4] How is this possible... how does adultery make a person guilty of violating the Sabbath? Sin occurs when we fail to love God or our neighbor as we are commanded.[5] If a man lusts after a woman, he is not loving God and his wife as he should. Even though he may be observing the law, the man is not fulfilling the law since he is guilty of selfishness. This is the point Jesus made.

1   Matthew 5:27-28
2   Exodus 25:16-22; Ezekiel 36:26; Hebrews 8:10-12
3   Romans 7:14
4   James 2:10
5   Matthew 22:37-40

The words of Jesus are a litmus test. If a man is tempted to look on a woman lustfully, he should understand that he is governed by the flesh. Lust violates the two laws of love and this is why lust is called "adultery within the heart." However, if this man is living **"in accordance with the Spirit have their** [he has his] **minds set on what the Spirit desires."**[1] A man's view of women is very different when he lives in accordance with the Spirit. Remember, the seventh commandment is a promise, a born-again heart will not commit adultery because love for God and neighbor will overcome temptation. Jesus has proven that love is more powerful than any temptation. **"For if you live according to the flesh, you will die; but if by the Spirit you put to death the misdeeds of the body, you will live. For those who are led by the Spirit of God are the children of God."**[2]

Paul Explains

Paul understood the difference between observing and fulfilling the law after meeting Jesus on the road to Damascus. He wrote, **"Once I was alive** [a self-righteous legalist, but I was actually living] **apart from** [the fulfillment of] **the law; but when** [the proper understanding of fulfilling] **the** [tenth] **commandment came** [to me]**, sin sprang to life** [I had to admit to myself that I had a covetous heart] **and I died** [that is, my self-righteousness was destroyed by this knowledge]. **I found that the very commandment that was intended to bring life** [by showing me what a heart of pure love will do] **actually brought death** [that is, it destroyed my self-righteousness and my arrogance – both had to die]."[3]

The bottom line is human beings cannot love as God loves unless the Holy Spirit generates God's love within. Obeying the Ten Commandments does not and cannot merit salvation. Sure, they will improve secular life if we obey them, but that is as far as they can go. On the other side of the coin, the Ten Commandments are a covenant

---

1   Romans 8:5, insertion mine
2   Romans 8:13-14; Genesis 39:10-13; Romans 7:14-20
3   Romans 7:9-10, insertions mine

showing born-again people what love for God and neighbor does.[1] Everyone will be tested during the Great Tribulation to see if they love God and neighbor wholeheartedly. Persecution will separate commandment *keepers* from commandment *fulfillers* because those fulfilling God's commandments will love Him more than they love their own lives! **"They triumphed over him** [the devil] **by the blood of the Lamb and by the word of their testimony; they did not love their lives so much as to shrink from death."**[2]

Meaningless Defense

If a person really wants to justify his or her rebellion against fulfilling the Ten Commandments, it is easy to lift various "sound bites" from their Scriptural context to support the notion. Peter noticed that Paul's writings were easy to distort when He wrote, **"Bear in mind that our Lord's patience means salvation, just as our dear brother Paul also wrote you with the wisdom that God gave him. He writes the same way in all his letters, speaking in them of these matters. His letters contain some things that are hard to understand, which ignorant and unstable people distort, as they do the other Scriptures, to their own destruction."**[3]

If this was true of Paul's epistles during the first century A.D., it is even truer today since we are far removed from the culture and problems associated with early Christians. If we casually lift segments of Paul's arguments in Galatians from their context, we can make Paul appear to say the opposite of what he is actually saying. I realize how easy this is because people often do this to me. Therefore, it is important when reading Paul's letters to read his whole argument carefully. This requires studying more than one of his books. Remember also, that prior to his conversion, Paul was highly educated and when he confronts various heresies entering Christianity through Jewish converts, he is using lessons from Israel's history to expose fatal flaws within Judaism.

---

1   James 1:12, 23-24
2   Revelation 12:11, insertion mine
3   2 Peter 3:15-16

Ephesians

Introduction

Paul wrote the book of Ephesians from a prison in Rome about A.D. 62. Most of the believers in Ephesus were Gentile converts. Jewish apologists were creating problems in Ephesus by advocating Jewish traditions, and Paul confronted their efforts with this epistle. Although these apologists had also caused problems in Galatia, Paul's tone in his letter to the Ephesians is not as abrasive as to the Galatians, but his counsel is just as wise and penetrating. As you consider Paul's counsel to the Ephesians, keep in mind that Jesus confronted the church at Ephesus 33 years later for having let go of its "first love" for Him.

The book of Ephesians has three main topics: First, Paul wanted the believers to know the Father predestined a time in world history when adopted Gentiles would be given the same rights as Jews without becoming Jewish! Second, Paul wanted the Ephesians to know Jesus gives spiritual gifts to all believers so His church will flourish. These gifts are recognized in servants of Jesus: apostles, prophets, evangelists, pastors, and teachers. Third, Paul wanted believers to know Jesus is glorified in His people when they reflect His holy character. Everyone professing to be a Christian should often read the last three chapters of Ephesians.

Competing Theories

Fatalism is a concept teaching "whatever will be, will be." There are variations of this concept, but the root of fatalism is everything that happens is predetermined and inevitable. Fatalism creates many questions and has few answers. On the other hand, predestination is a concept teaching that a higher power has mapped out every event in advance. There are no coincidences and each event has purpose and meaning, but like fatalism, what is its purpose? Of course, there are various understandings of predestination and it is ironic that the logical end to predestination is close to that of fatalism: "whatever has been predestined, will be."

One school of thought within predestination balances the Father's perfect foreknowledge, His divine purpose, and the free will of human beings. Paul does not explain this topic as well as John, but both Bible writers are in perfect harmony. Evidently there was some controversy about predestination in Ephesus and according to his style, Paul wasted no time jumping into the topic in Chapter 1. John and other Bible writers present information on predestination which Paul did not address. Once you properly understand the balance between God's foreknowledge, purpose, and the free will He gave us, Ephesians 1 and 2 will be easier to understand.

The Father Foreknew Everything

Any government has "top secret" information. Many corporations also have "top secret" information which they rigorously protect, because highly sensitive information can have unintended or harmful consequences if released. The Father is omniscient (all knowing). He foreknew Lucifer and his followers would rebel and be expelled from heaven before the angels were created. The Father foreknew the details surrounding the fall of Adam and Eve before Earth was created. He foreknew Cain would kill Abel. He foreknew Jesus' death on the cross; even the names and actions of the religious leaders and soldiers who participated in His death. All these details were included in a book which He wrote *before* the creation of the universe.

The Father included extremely sensitive information in His book which necessitates the utmost security until such time He wants it to be known. This explains why, after writing it, He physically sealed His book seven times. Looking thousands of years into the future, the Father foreknew who would choose to be saved from the penalty for sin and who would not. He foreknew the eternal destiny each angel would choose and recorded it before any of them were created. The Father also blotted out the *names* (but not the life record) of those who will be destroyed by fire at the end of the 1,000 years. His book will endure as a changeless testimony for all eternity.

Given the sensitive nature of this information, one may wonder why the Father would put it in writing. He foreknew if this information were exposed prematurely or fell into the hands of his adversaries, He would never escape taunts of ridicule and condemnation. The charges, "God is not a God of love" could be repeated throughout eternity because He *predestined* certain angels and certain humans to be saved and others destroyed. The charge would include, "He even wrote the results before they were created!" His adversaries would say, "Look! He is condemned by His own words! He created and manipulated His subjects according to His will. His subjects do not have free will, the power of choice, or any control over their destiny." There are obvious problems with these accusations; first and foremost, there is a great gulf between foreknowing and orchestrating.

The Father put the plan in motion to exonerate Himself from any hint of wrongdoing that could arise in the future. After writing the book and sealing it seven times, He stored it as a "time capsule" in heaven's vault. Then, at the dawn of Creation, certain angels were assigned to serve as recording angels. These angels were given special abilities to record one's life in real time: information revealed by the Holy Spirit who sees everything and reads the mind and heart of each person. These recordings include our motives, thoughts, knowledge, words, and actions—nothing is missed.

The Father predetermined three actions to make matters entirely transparent: First, because the curse of sin would make life unfair for human beings on Earth, each sinner would be given a generous opportunity for eternal life. Second, the Father predetermined that at an appointed time Jesus would, after dying on the cross which provided the righteousness needed for salvation, investigate the life record of each human. After reviewing each life record, Jesus would determine who would be saved and who would not. Third, the Father predetermined His book will be opened after two events: Jesus has to finish deciding who will be saved and lost and the saints have to finish deciding the amount of restitution the wicked must pay. Therefore, at the end of the 1,000 years, the Father's sealed book will finally be opened for everyone to see.

The Great White Throne Judgment

The Bible teaches that Jesus has been appointed to judge sinners. **"The Father judges no one, but has entrusted all judgment to the Son."**[1] Paul wrote, **"For we must all appear before the judgment seat of Christ, that each one may receive what is due us for the things done while in the body, whether good or bad."**[2] When our case comes before Jesus, He will see and review everything which the angels and Holy Spirit recorded: **"For God will bring every deed into judgment, including every hidden thing, whether it is good or evil."**[3]

The relationship between the records made by the recording angels and the book sealed with seven seals may surprise you. At the end of the 1,000 years, the saints who have been taken to heaven at the Second Coming will descend within the Holy City as it comes down from heaven. After the "dust settles," all the wicked will be resurrected so everyone who has ever lived on Earth will be alive and present at that moment. The total population of Earth from all ages, together with all of the angels including Lucifer and his angels, will be in attendance. Jesus and the Father will be seated on a high and glorious white throne that shines brighter than the sun. When everyone has gathered, Jesus will stand and a hush will fall over the innumerable host. Solemnity and sobriety will fill the atmosphere.

Our glorious Creator will call for the recordings made by the angels. The Bible calls the recordings "books." These books will be opened and, suddenly, all created beings will watch a vivid panorama. Each person will see a movie of his own life, including his motives, thoughts, words, and actions as they happened. Each being will also see his many responses to the Holy Spirit showing whether there was habitual submission or rebellion. As the movie continues, each

1   John 5:22
2   2 Corinthians 5:10
3   Ecclesiastes 12:14

person will see the Father's Plan of Salvation. The wicked angels will see the patience and grace extended to them in heaven before their rebellion reached the point of no return. Each human will see what the Father did to save repentant sinners. Everyone will see the birth, ministry, suffering, and death of Jesus when He came to Earth. All will be overwhelmed with God's love for sinners.

Finally, each angel and human being will learn about his eternal destiny. Each person will watch the process of his own judgment which occurred prior to the Second Coming. The angels were tested and judged before Earth was created. Each person will actually see the moment when Jesus examined his life and determined his destiny. Each person will observe the joy in heaven that followed during the judgment for those who were declared righteous and the sorrow for those who could not be saved. At the end of this panoramic presentation, all created beings (angels and humans alike) will fall to the ground before Jesus. The words of Isaiah will be fulfilled:

" 'By myself I have sworn, my mouth has uttered in all integrity a word that will not be revoked: Before me every knee will bow; by me every tongue will swear. They will say of me, "In the Lord alone are righteousness and strength." ' All who have raged against him will come to him and be put to shame. But all the descendants of Israel will find deliverance in the Lord and make their boast in him."[1]

The righteous within the Holy City will fall on their faces before Jesus saying something like this, "Lord Jesus! I can't believe you saved me! I do not deserve the gift of eternal life or even the lowest place in your kingdom. I am totally undone by your selfless sacrifice and the gift of your righteousness. Worthy, worthy, worthy is the Lamb of God who took away my sin. My salvation belongs to You, the Lamb of God who was slain for me."

The wicked outside the Holy City will also fall on their faces before Jesus saying something like this, "Lord God Almighty! Your judgment is righteous and true. The evidence is clear, the record is true, and your judgment is righteous. You have treated me generously.

---

1   Isaiah 45:23-25

You gave me life and opportunity. My repeated rebellion against the Holy Spirit was my own doing and I own the consequences of my behavior. I am a sinner without a Savior. I cannot change my sinful state. I am the person I chose to become."

Seventh Seal Broken

After "This is Your Life" movie has ended, Jesus will tell the numberless crowd to stand and He will approach a glorious table. He will lift up the huge book the Father wrote. This "Book of Life" will have just one seal remaining. After Jesus explains the origin and nature of the book, He will break open the final seal. Another movie lasting about one half hour will then occur. Everyone will gaze at a giant panorama in the sky and watch the contents of the book displayed! A great revelation will sweep over the crowd as everyone sees that the Father's book is *identical* to the books of records prepared by the Holy Spirit and the recording angels in real time. Amazingly, everyone will see the names of angels and human beings which were blotted out of the book even before they were created! This information is no longer sensitive since all judgment has been completed.

Each angel and person has already admitted to Jesus that His judgment was righteous and true. Each wicked angel and wicked human being will find his life record perfectly recorded in the Book of Life, but he will find his name blotted out! Each righteous person will also find his life perfectly recorded in the Book of Life, but his sins were blotted out by the righteousness of Jesus! All that remains is his name! What a stunning revelation! The Father foreknew, before created beings existed, who would choose to be inside or outside the Holy City.

Three Facts about Foreknowledge

Of course, volumes could be written on this matter, but there are three facts that can be distilled from this once-in-an-eternity moment. First, the Father will prove that His foreknowledge is perfect. Identical histories, one written before Creation and the other written in real time, will prove this fact. Second, because these histories are written, the Father will be exonerated from the accusation that He manipulated the eternal destiny of His subjects. While He foreknew the rise of sin, motives, thoughts, words, and actions of everyone, He also gave everyone free will and the liberty to exercise their freedom. He even emptied heaven's storehouse and paid the price for sin so each repentant sinner could have eternal life! Therefore, the presence of two groups standing before the throne, one saved and the other condemned, proves personal choice determined the eternal destiny for each individual.

Remember, by this time each angel and person has admitted that Jesus carefully and generously judged him in righteousness and truth. Everyone has already confessed that Jesus took into account everything possible in order to save to the utmost. Everyone knows firsthand that Jesus judged fairly. Ironically, the wicked are shut out of the Holy City because they chose to shut out the voice of the Holy Spirit; the righteous are inside the Holy City because they submitted to the voice of the Holy Spirit.

Third, it is important to understand that the Father does not judge anyone. He, as the author of the Book of Life, did not determine the eternal destiny of anyone. The Father appointed Jesus, who does not have foreknowledge, to be the judge of mankind. This is because Jesus has walked in our shoes. He knows what life is like on Earth as a human being and the Father ordained that human beings would be judged by someone who was tempted in all points as sinners are and who overcame every temptation. This is both righteous and fair. Additionally, the Father has not permitted Jesus to know what is written in the "Book of Life." As our judge, Jesus has to examine each person's record on its own merit. The Father ordained that Jesus must judge the record of each person's life before millions of watching angels as intelligent, reasoning witnesses. The Father did this because He wants the holy angels to understand His judicial system, and to observe how deliberate, careful, and generous Jesus is in judging every case.

Remember, these angels will live with the Father and Jesus throughout eternity. Therefore, if trust, faith, and love for God and His government are to endure forever, the Father and Jesus must do everything in open and transparent ways. Not even the slightest hint of inappropriate behavior can be found in God's ways, or given enough time such knowledge could fester into another rebellion.

Think about this: If Jesus had foreknowledge and knew what the Father had written, and Jesus' judgments perfectly aligned with what the Father wrote, everyone would suspect a scam. The judgment of sinners would be a charade. The Father and Son would be co-conspirators, one defending the other by making the written predictions come true. Most of all, if this were the case, the devil and his followers would be exonerated for rebelling against the Father and Jesus!

Foreknowledge Is Not Predestination

Many people have trouble separating God's foreknowledge from predestination. If a person sets the alarm on the clock for 6 P.M., he predestines the alarm to sound at 6 P.M. If another person enters the room and sees the clock alarm is set for 6 P.M., he has foreknowledge, but his foreknowledge has nothing to do with causing the event to happen. Because the Father has perfect foreknowledge, He predestined events to occur before the creation of the universe including the wonderful plan to save repentant sinners. However, the Father has predestined no one's eternal destiny. This is vitally important! The Father sets times and dates for events by His own authority, and He has predestined the fulfillment of certain purposes and plans. However, He works through beings who have free will and the power of choice. **"The Spirit and the bride say, 'Come!' And let the one who hears say, 'Come!' Let the one who is thirsty come; and let the one who wishes take the free gift of the water of life."**[1] Once you understand that the Father's purposes and corporate plans are one thing and our response to the Holy Spirit is our choice, the topics of God's foreknowledge and predestination come together in perfect harmony.

Paul addresses foreknowledge and predestination in the first part of his epistle to the church at Ephesus. As you read, look for what the Father has predestined and the result that follows if a person *chooses* to follow the prompting of the Holy Spirit.

---

1   Revelation 22:17

Ephesians Chapter 1

Ephesians 1:1-3: "**Paul, an apostle of Christ Jesus by the will of God, To God's holy people in Ephesus,** [who remain steadfast and are] **the faithful in Christ Jesus: Grace and peace to you from God our Father and the Lord Jesus Christ. Praise be to the God and Father of our Lord Jesus Christ, who has blessed us** [from his throne] **in the heavenly realms with every spiritual blessing in** [through] **Christ.**"

Ephesians 1:4-6: "[Foreknowing the curse of sin and that all have sinned] **For he** [the Father] **chose** [to make] **us** [who believe] **in him** [Jesus] **before the creation of the world to be** [made] **holy and blameless in his sight. In love he predestined us** [sinners] **for** [redemption and] **adoption to** [legal] **sonship through Jesus Christ, in accordance with his pleasure and will – to the praise of his glorious grace, which he has freely given us in the One he loves** [Jesus, the Lamb of God]."

Ephesians 1:7-10: "**In him** [Jesus] **we** [sinners] **have redemption through his blood, the forgiveness of sins, in accordance with the riches of God's grace that he** [the Father] **lavished on us. With all wisdom and understanding, he** [the Father has] **made known to us** [believers in Jesus] **the mystery of his will** [through Israel's prophets] **according to his good pleasure, which he purposed in** [through] **Christ** [before the world was created], **to be put into effect when the times reach their fulfillment –** [The Father predestined before the world was created that at an appointed time, he would put everything] **to bring unity to all things in heaven and on earth under Christ.**"

Paul mentions an event that few people appreciate. The Father predetermined before the world was created, that in 1798, Jesus would be revealed in heaven as an equal of the Father by putting everything in heaven and on Earth under Jesus' control. The knowledge of His plan, called *The Revelation of Jesus Christ,* has been slowly advancing on Earth ever since. During the Great Tribulation, the revelation of all that Jesus is will dramatically unfold for the world to see.

The Father wants the universe to know that Jesus is a self-existing God; He has all the powers and prerogatives of deity just like Himself. This matter is very important to understand because other than His time on the Father's throne, Jesus lives in subjection to the Father. At the end of the 1,000 years, Jesus will step down from the Father's throne and once again live in subjection to the Father.

Consider Paul's words: *"For as in Adam all die, so in Christ all will be made alive. But each in turn: Christ, the firstfruits; then, when he comes, those who belong to him. Then the end will come, when he [Jesus] hands over the kingdom to God the Father after he has destroyed all dominion, authority and power. For he must reign until he has put all his enemies under his feet. The last enemy to be destroyed is death. For he 'has [set a time to] put everything under his feet.' Now when it says that 'everything' has been put under him [Jesus], it is clear that this does not include God himself, who put everything under Christ. When he [Jesus] has done this [destroyed death itself], then the Son himself will be made subject to him who put everything under him, so that God [the Father] may be all in all."*[1]

Ephesians 1:11-12: **"In him** [Jesus] **we** [Jews, the offspring of Abraham] **were also chosen, having been predestined** [selected] **according to the plan of him who works out everything in conformity with the purpose of his will, in order that we** [Jewish converts]**, who were the first to put our** [find the] **hope** [of salvation] **in** [through] **Christ, might be for the praise of his glory."**

Ephesians 1:13-17: **"And you** [Gentile believers] **also were included in Christ when you heard the message of truth, the gospel of your salvation. When you believed** [in God's Son]**, you were marked in him with a seal,** [and your adoption as sons was manifested by] **the promised Holy Spirit, who is a deposit guaranteeing our inheritance until the** [day of] **redemption** [occurs. All who follow Jesus are] **of those who are God's**

---

1   1 Corinthians 15:22-28, insertions and italics mine

possession – to the praise of his glory. For this reason, ever since I heard about your faith in the Lord Jesus and your love for all God's people, I have not stopped giving thanks for you, remembering you in my prayers. I keep asking that the God of our Lord Jesus Christ, the glorious Father, may give you the Spirit of wisdom and revelation, so that you may know him better."

Ephesians 1:18-23: "I pray that the eyes of your heart may be enlightened in order that you may know [and understand] the hope to which he has called you, the riches of his glorious inheritance in [for] his holy people, and his incomparably great power for us who believe. That power is the same as the mighty strength he exerted when he raised Christ from the dead and seated him at his right hand in the heavenly realms, far above all rule and authority, power and dominion, and every name that is invoked, not only in the present age but also in the one to come. And God [our Father has] placed all things under his [Christ's] feet and appointed him to be head over everything for the church, which is his body, the fullness of him who fills everything in every way."

Ephesians Chapter 2

Ephesians 2:1-3: "[Now, dear brothers, I need to address a spiritual matter that is racial and inflammatory in nature.] **As for** [all of] **you,** [there was a time when]**, you were dead in your transgressions and sins** [that is, you were spiritually dead, unaware of your true condition before God and unaware of God's amazing grace and truth, the ministry of the Holy Spirit, or the Father's love manifested for sinners through the ministry and death of Jesus]**, in which you used to live** [according to your carnal instincts and sinful desires] **when you followed the ways of this world and of** [Lucifer] **the ruler of the kingdom of the air,** [he is] **the** [demonic] **spirit who is now at work in those who are** [spiritually dead and] **disobedient. All of us also lived among them** [and like them – the pagans] **at one time,** [we lived] **gratifying the cravings of our flesh** [sinful nature] **and following its desires and thoughts. Like the rest, we were by nature deserving of** [God's coming] **wrath** [for wickedness]."

Ephesians 2:4-7: **"But because of his great love for us, God** [the Father], **who is rich in mercy,** [changed us. Through the gospel of Jesus and the power of the Holy Spirit, He] **made us alive with Christ even when we were dead in transgressions** – [therefore, you must never forget that] **it is by** [His] **grace you have been saved. And God** [the Father] **raised us up** [from the dead – spiritually speaking] **with Christ and seated us** [as sons – spiritually speaking] **with him in the heavenly realms in** [through] **Christ Jesus, in order that in the coming ages** [after the drama with sin ends] **he might** [forever] **show the incomparable riches of his grace, expressed in his kindness to us in** [through] **Christ Jesus."**

Ephesians 2:8-9: **"For it is by grace you have been saved** [made alive spiritually], **through faith** [in Jesus] – **and this** [power] **is** [did] **not** [come] **from** [within] **yourselves** [you did not raise yourself from the dead], **it** [the spiritual life you now have] **is the gift of God – not by works** [no one can possibly do this on his own], **so that no one can boast."**

Ephesians 2:10-12: **"For we** [Jews and Gentiles alike] **are God's handiwork, created in Christ Jesus to do good works** [for one another], **which God prepared in advance** [predetermined] **for us to do. Therefore, remember that formerly you who are Gentiles by birth and called** [ridiculed as] **'uncircumcised' by** [the apologists, are no different than] **those who call themselves** [boast they are] **'the circumcision' (which** [the circumcision of which the Jews boast] **is done in the body by human hands)** – [and we know this is now meaningless. Also] **remember that at that time** [before Jesus died or you heard about Him] **you were separate from Christ, excluded from citizenship in Israel and foreigners** [ignorant of] **to the covenants of the promise** [which God gave to and through Israel], **without hope**

and without God in the world. [In other words, before you Gentiles heard about Jesus, you were nothing and had nothing – spiritually speaking.]"

Ephesians 2:13-16: "But now in Christ Jesus you who once were far away have been brought near [to the Father] by [through] the blood of Christ. For he himself is our peace, who has made the two groups [races into] one and has destroyed the [religious] barrier, the dividing wall of hostility [that kept us apart], by setting aside [abolishing] in his flesh the [Levitical] law with its commands and regulations [the laws which formerly made us two separate and distinct races]. His purpose [with the new covenant] was to create in himself one new humanity out of the two [races], thus making peace [between us], and in one body [the body of Jesus] to reconcile both of them [both races] to God through the cross, by which he put to death their hostility [Jesus abolished the Levitical system which terminated the racial/spiritual divide]."

Ephesians 2:17-22: "He [Jesus] came and preached peace to you [Gentiles] who were far away [from his gospel] and peace to those [Jews] who were near [to his gospel, but were nevertheless steeped in tradition and ignorance]. For through him [Jesus] we both have access to the Father by one Spirit. Consequently, you [Gentiles] are no longer foreigners and strangers, but fellow citizens with God's people and members of his household [Christ's church which is], built on the foundation of the apostles and prophets, with Christ Jesus himself as the chief cornerstone. In him the whole building [all people] is [are] joined together [as one body] and [his church] rises to become a holy temple in the Lord. And in him you too are being built together [with the rest of the believers] to become a dwelling in which God lives by his Spirit."

Ephesians Chapter 3

Ephesians 3:1-3: "For this reason I, Paul, the prisoner of Christ
Jesus for the sake of you Gentiles – Surely you have heard
about the administration of God's grace that was given to me
for you, that is, the mystery made known to me by revelation
[from Jesus], as I have already written briefly."

Ephesians 3:4-9: "In reading this [epistle], then, you will be able
to understand my insight into the mystery of Christ, which
was not made known to people in other generations as it
has now been revealed by the Spirit to God's holy apostles
and prophets. This mystery is that through the gospel the
Gentiles are heirs together with Israel, members together
of one body, and sharers together in the promise in Christ
Jesus. I became a servant of this gospel by the gift of God's
grace given me through the working of his power. Although
I am less than the least of all the Lord's people, this grace
was given me: to preach to the Gentiles the boundless
[infinite] riches of Christ, and to make plain to everyone the
administration of this mystery, which for ages past was kept
hidden in God [but was predestined by the Father to be exposed
at this time], who created [designed] all things."

Ephesians 3:10-12: "His intent was that now, through the church,
the manifold wisdom of God should be made known [also] to
the rulers and authorities [the angels] in the heavenly realms,
according to his eternal purpose that he accomplished in
Christ Jesus our Lord. In him and through faith in him we
may approach God with freedom and confidence."

Ephesians 3:13-19: "I ask you, therefore, not to be discouraged
because of my sufferings for you, which are your glory. For
this reason I kneel before the Father, from whom every family
in heaven and on earth derives its name. I pray that out of his
glorious riches he may strengthen you with power through
his Spirit in your inner being, so that Christ may dwell in
your hearts through faith. And I pray that you, being rooted

and established in love, may have power, together with all the Lord's holy people, to grasp how wide and long and high and deep is the love of Christ, and to know this love that surpasses knowledge – that you may be filled to the measure of all the fullness of God."

Ephesians 3:20-21: "Now to him who is able to do immeasurably more than all we ask or imagine, according to his power that is at work within us, to him be glory in the church and in Christ Jesus throughout all generations, for ever and ever! Amen."

Ephesians Chapter 4

Ephesians 4:1-3: "As a prisoner for the Lord, then, I urge you to live a life worthy of the calling you have received. Be completely humble and gentle; be patient, bearing with one another in love. Make every effort to keep the unity of the Spirit through the bond of peace."

Ephesians 4:4-10: "There is one body and one Spirit, just as you were called to one hope when you were called; one Lord, one faith, one baptism; one God and Father of all, who is over all and through all and in all. But to each one of us grace has been given as Christ apportioned it. This is why it says: 'When he ascended on high, he took many captives and gave gifts to his people.' (What does 'he ascended' mean except that he also descended to the lower, earthly regions? He who descended is the very one who ascended higher than all the heavens, in order to fill the whole universe [with the glory of the Father].)"

Paul quotes a Messianic prophecy found in Psalm 68: **"When you ascended on high, you took many captives; you received gifts from people, even from the rebellious** [sinners] **– that you, Lord God, might dwell there."**[1] Paul is bringing up the point that when Jesus died, many people were resurrected: **"At that moment the**

---

1   Psalm 68:18, insertion mine

curtain of the temple was torn in two from top to bottom. The earth shook, the rocks split and the tombs broke open. The bodies of many holy people who had died were raised to life. They came out of the tombs after Jesus' resurrection and went into the holy city and appeared to many people."[1]

The Father commanded this special resurrection. To overcome the lies of the Pharisees that the disciples had stolen Jesus' body, the Father raised dead people to prove that resurrection was possible. The Father also raised dead people so Jesus could present Himself with these saints as firstfruits from the dead. Finally, the Father raised these dead people so 24 of them (described in the book of Revelation as 24 elders) could serve in heaven's court.

Therefore, when Jesus ascended, He led "many captives" as He approached the Father. These captives were formerly dead people, that is, "captives liberated from their tombs." The 24 elders were chosen from this group and were given a high honor in heaven to serve as witnesses during Christ's judgment of mankind. Since there are 12 tribes, two elders were chosen from each tribe making 24 witnesses. The title "elder" means "someone ordained by God to serve his brothers and sisters." Therefore, after eternity begins and if a saint questions why someone was not saved, two witnesses will affirm the fairness and transparency of Christ's verdict.

Ephesians 4:11-13: "[It was customary in Bible times for a victorious king returning from war to show his love and affection for his people by generously giving them gifts as he paraded his troops through the city. Jesus did something similar at his ascension. After He had overcome every temptation and cast Lucifer out of heaven, Jesus gave generous gifts to His believers on Earth.] **So Christ himself gave** [some people to be] **the apostles, the prophets, the evangelists, the pastors and teachers, to equip his people for works of service, so that the body of Christ may be built up until we all reach unity in the faith and in the knowledge of the Son of God**

---

1   Matthew 27:51-53

and become mature, attaining to the whole measure of the fullness of Christ."

Ephesians 4:14-15: "Then we will no longer be infants, tossed back and forth by the waves, and blown here and there by every wind of teaching and by the cunning and craftiness of people in their deceitful scheming. Instead, speaking the truth in love, we will grow to become in every respect the mature body of him who is the head, that is, Christ."

Ephesians 4:16-19: "From him the whole body, joined and held together by every supporting ligament, grows and builds itself up in love, as each part does its work. So I tell you this, and insist on it in the Lord, that you [who were formerly Gentiles] must no longer live as the Gentiles do, in the futility of their thinking. They are darkened in their understanding and separated from the life of God because of the ignorance that is in them due to the hardening of their hearts. Having lost all sensitivity, they have given themselves over to sensuality so as to indulge in every kind of impurity, and they are full of greed."

Ephesians 4:20-24: "That, however, is not the way of life you learned when you heard about Christ and were taught in him in accordance with the truth that is in Jesus. You were taught, with regard to your former way of life, to put off your old self, which is being corrupted by its deceitful desires; to be made new in the attitude of your minds; and to put on the new self, created to be like God in true righteousness and holiness."

Ephesians 4:25-30: "Therefore each of you must put off falsehood and speak truthfully to your neighbor, for we are all members of one body. 'In your anger do not sin': Do not let the sun go down while you are still angry, and do not give the devil a foothold. Anyone who has been stealing must steal no longer, but must work, doing something useful with their own hands, that they may have something to share with those in need. Do not let any unwholesome talk come out of your mouths, but only what is helpful for building others up according to their needs, that it may benefit those who listen. And do not grieve the Holy Spirit of God, with whom you were sealed for the day of redemption."

Ephesians 4:31-32: "Get rid of all bitterness, rage and anger, brawling and slander, along with every form of malice. Be kind and compassionate to one another, forgiving each other, just as in Christ God forgave you."

Ephesians Chapter 5

Ephesians 5:1-3: "Follow God's example, therefore, as dearly loved children and walk in the way of love, just as Christ loved us and gave himself up for us as a fragrant offering and sacrifice to God. But among you there must not be even a hint of sexual immorality, or of any kind of impurity, or of greed, because these are improper for God's holy people."

Ephesians 5:4-7: "Nor should there be obscenity, foolish talk or coarse joking, which are out of place, but rather thanksgiving. For of this you can be sure: No immoral, impure or greedy person – such a person is an idolater – has any inheritance in the kingdom of Christ and of God. Let no one deceive you with empty words, for because of such things God's wrath comes on those who are disobedient. Therefore do not be partners with them."

Ephesians 5:8-12: "For you were once darkness, but now you are light in the Lord. Live as children of light (for the fruit of the light consists in all goodness, righteousness and truth) and find out what pleases the Lord. Have nothing to do with the fruitless deeds of darkness, but rather expose them. It is shameful even to mention what the disobedient do in secret."

Ephesians 5:13-16: "But everything exposed by the light becomes visible – and everything that is illuminated becomes a light. This is why it is said: 'Wake up, sleeper, rise from the dead, and Christ will shine on you.' Be very careful, then, how you live – not as unwise but as wise, making the most of every opportunity, because the days are [full of] evil."

Ephesians 5:17-20: "Therefore do not be foolish, but understand what the Lord's will is. Do not get drunk on wine, which leads to debauchery. Instead, be filled with the Spirit, speaking to one another with psalms, hymns, and songs from the Spirit. Sing and make music from your heart to the Lord, always giving thanks to God the Father for everything, in the name of our Lord Jesus Christ."

Ephesians 5:21-27: "Submit to one another out of reverence for Christ. Wives, submit yourselves to your own husbands as you do to the Lord. For the husband is the head of the wife as Christ is the head of the church, his body, of which he is the Savior. Now as the church submits to Christ, so also wives should submit to their husbands in everything. Husbands, love your wives, just as Christ loved the church and gave himself up for her to make her holy, cleansing her by the washing with water through the word, and to present her to himself as a radiant church, without stain or wrinkle or any other blemish, but holy and blameless."

Ephesians 5:28-33: "In this same way, husbands ought to love their wives as their own bodies. He who loves his wife loves himself. After all, no one ever hated their own body, but they feed and care for their body, just as Christ does the church – for we are members of his body. 'For this reason a man will leave his father and mother and be united to his wife, and the two will become one flesh.' This is a profound mystery – but I am talking about Christ and the church. However, each one of you also must love his wife as he loves himself, and the wife must respect her husband."

Ephesians Chapter 6

Ephesians 6:1-4: "Children, obey your parents in the Lord, for this is right. 'Honor your father and mother' – which is the first commandment with a promise – 'so that it may go well with you and that you may enjoy long life on the earth.' Fathers, do not exasperate your children; instead, bring them up in the training and instruction of the Lord."

Ephesians 6:5-9: "Slaves, obey your earthly masters with respect and fear, and with sincerity of heart, just as you would obey Christ. Obey them not only to win their favor when their eye is on you, but as slaves of Christ, doing the will of God from your heart. Serve wholeheartedly, as if you were serving the Lord, not people, because you know that the Lord will reward each one for whatever good they do, whether they are slave or free. And masters, treat your slaves in the same way. Do not threaten them, since you know that he who is both their Master and yours is in heaven, and there is no favoritism with him."

Ephesians 6:10-12: "Finally, be strong in the Lord and in his mighty power. Put on the full armor of God, so that you can take your stand against the devil's schemes. For our struggle is not against flesh and blood, but against the rulers, against the authorities, against the powers of this dark world and against the spiritual forces of evil in the heavenly realms."

Ephesians 6:13-17: "Therefore put on the full armor of God, so that when the day of evil comes, you may be able to stand your ground, and after you have done everything, to stand. Stand firm then, with the belt of truth buckled around your waist, with the breastplate of righteousness in place, and with your feet fitted with the readiness that comes from the gospel of peace. In addition to all this, take up the shield of faith, with which you can extinguish all the flaming arrows of the evil one. Take the helmet of salvation and the sword of the Spirit, which is the word of God."

Ephesians 6:18-20: "And pray in the Spirit on all occasions with all kinds of prayers and requests. With this in mind, be alert and always keep on praying for all the Lord's people. Pray also for me, that whenever I speak, words may be given me so that I will fearlessly make known the mystery of the gospel, for which I am an ambassador in chains. Pray that I may declare it fearlessly, as I should."

Ephesians 6:21-24: "Tychicus, the dear brother and faithful servant in the Lord, will tell you everything [when he delivers this letter], so that you also may know how I am and what I am doing. I am sending him to you for this very purpose, that you may know how we are, and that he may encourage you. Peace to the brothers and sisters, and love with faith from God the Father and the Lord Jesus Christ. Grace to all who love our Lord Jesus Christ with an undying love."

Colossians

Introduction

Paul wrote this epistle when he was in prison about A.D. 62. The church at Colossae was located in Asia Minor, and primarily consisted of Gentile converts who came to know Christ through the ministry of Epaphras–a Greek convert. Paul did not visit this church. The Romans were persecuting the Jews and problems began when Jewish apologists attended the church and challenged the gospel which Epaphras taught. Epaphras told Paul about it and this epistle was his handwritten response.

The epistle to the Colossians closely parallels those which Paul wrote to Galatia and Ephesus. If you lay these three epistles side-by-side and study their outlines, you will be surprised at the similarity, even parallelism between them. The parallelism occurs because Paul was constantly challenged by Jewish apologists about the same four topics.

a. The Jews did not accept the deity of Jesus. Jewish monotheism does not allow for more than one God.[1]

b. The Jews insisted the Gentiles must be circumcised. Paul taught circumcision was abolished at the cross because God had made a "new man" out of the two groups of people. This new man did not need fleshly circumcision because the hearts of born-again believers in Christ had already been circumcised! **"A person is not a Jew who is one only outwardly, nor is circumcision merely outward and physical. No, a person is a Jew who is one inwardly; and circumcision is circumcision of the heart, by the Spirit, not by the written code. Such a person's praise is not from other people, but from God."[2] "For he himself is our peace, who has made the two groups** [Jews and Gentiles] **one and has destroyed the barrier, the dividing wall of hostility, by setting aside in his flesh the law with its commands and regulations. His purpose was to create in himself one new**

---

1   For further study, see *wake-up.org/pauls-conversion-information*
2   Romans 2:28-29

humanity out of the two, thus making peace, and in one body to reconcile both of them to God through the cross, by which he put to death their hostility."[1]

c. The Jews taught that salvation is only possible through obedience to all of the laws of God and Moses. Paul taught that the law of God is spiritual, and the intent of the law is only fulfilled through love. Moreover, salvation comes through faith, not through works.[2]

d. Paul insisted that love for God (meaning submission to) and neighbor (meaning humble to) is essential in God's sight. The apologists insisted the Old Testament was sufficient in matters of doctrine and observing Israel's long-standing traditions was of paramount importance.[3]

Contrary to what many Christians believe about Colossians 2, there is no discussion within the New Testament concerning the sacredness and observance of God's seventh day Sabbath after the cross. I believe there is total silence on this topic because there was no question about its validity. Paul wrote Colossians 2 about thirty years after the cross, and if the fourth commandment had been abolished, we can be sure the Jewish apologists would have constantly argued with Paul on this topic. Everyone who uses Colossians 2 to justify the abolishment of the fourth commandment are distorting Paul's words, putting the Bible in a state of internal conflict, and denigrating our Creator's generous gift to man.[4]

To be clear, there is conflict in Galatians, Ephesians, Colossians, and Romans between Paul and Jewish apologists over circumcision, food offered to idols, the observance of new moon feasts, and the five feasts: Passover, Pentecost, Trumpets, Day of Atonement, and Tabernacles. To understand the conflict, it is important to understand that the five feasts Israel observed were also called "sabbaths."[5]

---

1   Ephesians 2:14-16, insertion mine; For further study see commentary on Galatians 4 & 5; Ephesians 2.
2   For further study, see *wake-up.org/pauls-conversion-information*
3   For further study, see pp. 7-8, 15-21, 22-30, and *wake-up.org/pauls-conversion-information*
4   Mark 2:27-28
5   See Leviticus 16:31 on the Day of Atonement.

These irregular sabbaths occurred throughout the weekly cycle–like our birthdays–according to the calendar.

Paul wrote in Colossians 2 that the Levitical code was nailed to the cross. He meant that circumcision, new moon feasts, the five feast days, and many other requirements pertaining to eating or drinking,[1] were abolished at the cross. Paul wrote in Galatians 5:3 it is foolish to think a person can observe some of the law and not carry out *all* of the law's demands. For example, it is impossible to observe the whole law and keep Passover without killing a lamb at the specified time in the specified manner. Since the prophecy and promise embedded in the Passover has been fulfilled through Jesus (the Lamb of God has been slain, resurrected, and seated at the right hand of the Father as our High Priest), the whole law concerning Passover had to be abolished at the cross.

Colossians Chapter 1

Colossians 1:1-2: "Paul, an apostle of Christ Jesus by the will of God, and Timothy our brother, To God's holy people in Colossae, the faithful brothers and sisters in Christ: Grace and peace to you from God our Father."

Colossians 1:3-6: "We always thank God, the Father of our Lord Jesus Christ, when we pray for you, because we have heard of your faith in Christ Jesus and of the love you have for all God's people—the faith and love that spring from the hope stored up for you in heaven and about which you have already heard in the true message of the gospel that has come to you. In the same way, the gospel is bearing fruit and growing throughout the whole world [given Paul's world view]**—just as it has been doing among you since the day you heard it and truly understood God's grace."**

Colossians 1:7-12: "You learned it [the gospel] **from Epaphras, our dear fellow servant, who is a faithful minister of Christ**

---

[1] Fasting was regarded as an outward show of piety. Zechariah 7:4-7; Matthew 6:16-17; 9:14-15; 11:18-19. See fasting on Purim, Esther 9:31

on our behalf, and who also told us of your love in the Spirit. For this reason, since the day we heard about you, we have not stopped praying for you. We continually ask God to fill you with the knowledge of his will through all the wisdom and understanding that the Spirit gives, so that you may live a life worthy of the Lord and please him in every way: bearing fruit in every good work, growing in the knowledge of God, being strengthened with all power according to his glorious might so that you may have great endurance and patience, and giving joyful thanks to the Father, who has qualified you to share in the inheritance of his holy people in the kingdom of light."

Colossians 1:13-15: "**For he has rescued us from the dominion of darkness and brought us into the kingdom of the Son he loves, in** [through] **whom we have redemption, the forgiveness of sins. The Son** [Jesus] **is the image of the invisible God** [the Father], [Jesus is] **the firstborn over all creation.**"

Colossians 1:16: "**For in him** [Jesus] **all things were created: things in heaven and on earth, visible and invisible, whether thrones or powers or rulers or authorities; all things have been created through him and for him** [the Father – Hebrews 1:2]."

Colossians 1:17-20: "**He** [Jesus] **is before all things, and in him all things hold together. And he is the head of the body, the church; he is the beginning and** [the end,] **the firstborn** [the Preeminent One] **from among the dead, so that in everything he might have the supremacy. For God** [the Father] **was pleased to have all his fullness dwell in him** [On the Mount of Transfiguration, the deity of Jesus was exposed. He is an equal of the Father, a point which the apologists would not and could not accept]**, and through him**[, Jesus, the Father moved] **to reconcile to himself all things, whether things on earth or things** [the remaining angels] **in heaven, by making peace through his blood, shed on the cross.**"

Colossians 1:21-23: "**Once you** [Gentiles] **were** [in ignorance] **alienated from God and were enemies in your minds because** of your evil behavior. **But now he has reconciled you by Christ's physical body through death to present you holy in his sight, without blemish and free from accusation— if you continue in your faith, established and firm, and do not move from the hope held out in the gospel.** [Notice the importance of the word "if" in the previous sentence.] **This is the gospel that you heard** [from me and then Epaphras] **and that has been proclaimed to every creature under heaven** [not completed, but the gospel of Jesus was and is in the process of being proclaimed to every creature], **and of which I, Paul, have become a servant.**"

Colossians 1:24-26: "**Now I rejoice in what I am suffering for you, and I fill up in my flesh what is still lacking in regard to Christ's afflictions, for the sake of his body, which is the church. I have become its servant by the commission God gave me to present to you the word of God in its fullness—** [indicating the apologists do not have the whole story to tell] **the mystery that has been kept hidden for ages and generations, but is now disclosed to the Lord's people.** [This mystery is something the apologists could not understand.]"[1]

Colossians 1:27: "**To them** [the saints] **God has chosen to make known among the Gentiles the glorious riches of this mystery, which is Christ in you, the hope of glory.** ['Christ in you' was a foreign concept at the time, the notion that a God would live within an ordinary human being was shocking! Moreover, this concept meant there is no difference between Jew and Gentile in God's sight. The elect of God can be anyone, for Christ is eager to justify any repentant sinner and dwell within any willing person.]"

Colossians 1:28-29: "**He** [Jesus] **is the one we** [do not hesitate to] **proclaim, admonishing and teaching everyone with all wisdom, so that we may present everyone fully mature in Christ. To this end I strenuously contend with all the energy Christ so powerfully works in me.**"

---

1   Colossians 2:2; Ephesians 3; Galatians 1:11-12; Romans 16:25

Colossians Chapter 2

Colossians 2:1-3: "I want you to know how hard I am contending for you and for those at Laodicea, and for all who have not met me personally. My goal is that they may be encouraged in heart and united in love, so that they may have the full riches of complete understanding, in order that they may know the mystery of God, namely, Christ, in whom are hidden all the treasures of wisdom and knowledge. [Paul presents Jesus in a way that robs the apologists of their argument. The apologists were trying to get the believers at Colosse (mostly Gentile converts) to observe Jewish traditions in order to be saved and Paul ends their argument with the exposure of a mystery that abolishes Judaism – a mystery which the Jews did not and would not understand.]"

Colossians 2:4-7: "I tell you this so that no one may deceive you by fine-sounding arguments. For though I am absent from you in body, I am present with you in spirit and delight to see how disciplined you are and how firm your faith in Christ is. So then, just as you received Christ Jesus as Lord, continue to live your lives in him, rooted and built up in him, strengthened in the faith as you were taught, and overflowing with thankfulness."

Colossians 2:8-10: "See to it that no one takes you captive through hollow and deceptive philosophy, which depends on human [Jewish] **tradition and the elemental spiritual forces of this world** [driven by ego and ignorance] **rather than on Christ.** [Do not consider for a moment that Jesus was an ordinary man as the apologists would have you believe.] **For in Christ all the fullness of the Deity lives in bodily form,**[1] **and in Christ you have been brought to fullness. He is the head over every power and authority."**[2]

Colossians 2:11-12: "In him you were also circumcised with a circumcision not performed by human hands [and not in the

---

1   1 John 5:20
2   Matthew 28:18

flesh]. **Your whole self**[1] **ruled by the flesh was put off when you were circumcised by Christ, having been buried with him in baptism, in which you were also raised with him through your faith in the working of God, who raised him from the dead."**

Colossians 2:13-14: "When you were dead in your sins [unaware of God's love and will] **and in the uncircumcision of your flesh, God** [sent the Holy Spirit and through Him, He] **made you alive with Christ. He forgave us all our sins, having canceled the charge** [the Levitical laws] **of our legal indebtedness, which stood against us and condemned us;** [so because Jesus died] **he** [God the Father] **has taken it** [the Levitical code] **away, nailing it to the cross."**

Paul states the Levitical code condemned the Jews because laws cannot bring about a change of heart! Even the apologists had to admit that time after time, Israel had abandoned God because His ways proved to be too heavy a burden for Israel's carnal ways and hearts. Paul wrote in Romans 8:5-8: **"Those who live according to the flesh have their minds set on what the flesh desires; but those who live in accordance with the Spirit have their minds set on what the Spirit desires. The mind governed by the flesh is death, but the mind governed by the Spirit is life and peace. The mind governed by the flesh is hostile to God; it does not submit to God's law, nor can it do so. Those who are in the realm of the flesh cannot please God."**[2]

Colossians 2:15: "And having disarmed [neutralized] **the powers** [of Israel's laws] **and authorities** [such as the priesthood and the Pharisees]**, he made a public spectacle of them** [of their foolishness and insufficiency by having Jesus cleanse the temple twice and then, ripping the veil in the temple open, showing darkness was the only element within the Most Holy Place, the center of Israel's theology. The Father proved the end of

---

1   Romans 2:28-29
2   For further information, see *wake-up.org/pauls-conversion-information*

the Levitical code], **triumphing over them by the cross** [by making Jesus, who doesn't come from the tribe of Levi, but from the tribe of Judah, High Priest!]."[1]

Colossians 2:16: "Therefore do not let anyone [especially the apologists] **judge you** [condemn you] **by what you eat or drink,**[2] **or with regard to a religious festival** [required by the Levitical code], **a New Moon celebration or a Sabbath day** [required by Levitical law]."

The feast days were also considered holy or sabbath days, although they were never confused with seventh day Sabbath. The Day of Atonement was a sabbath day that fell on different days of the weekly cycle.[3] When a feast day and a seventh day Sabbath aligned, that day was recognized as a special Sabbath or a "high Sabbath."[4]

Colossians 2:17: "These [matters such as eating, drinking, and religious festivals] **are a shadow** [a template foretelling[5]] **of the things that were to come; the reality** [the meaning and fulfillment], **however, is found in Christ."**

For example, the feast of Passover points back in time to when Jesus passed over Egypt and investigated every house to see if blood had been applied to the door posts. This feast points forward to a time when Jesus, our High Priest and Judge, will pass over and investigate every heart to see if the sinner has applied His blood to the doorposts of his heart.[6]

Colossians 2:18-19: "Do not let anyone who delights in false humility and the worship of angels disqualify you. Such a person also goes into great detail about what they have seen [claiming a divine revelation from God]; **they are puffed up with idle notions by their unspiritual mind. They have lost**

---

1   Hebrews 7
2   Fasting was regarded as an outward show of piety. Zechariah 7:4-7; Matthew 6:16-17; 9:14-15; 11:18-19. See fasting on Purim, Esther 9:31
3   Leviticus 16:31
4   John 19:31 For further study on the perpetuity of the fourth commandment after the cross, see *wake-up.org/pauls-conversion-information*
5   Hebrews 8:1-5; 10:1
6   2 Corinthians 5:10; Ecclesiastes 12:13-14

connection with the head [Jesus], **from whom the whole body, supported and held together by its ligaments and sinews, grows as God causes it to grow."**

Colossians 2:20-22: "Since you died with Christ to the elemental spiritual forces of this world [when you first believed], **why, as though you still belonged to the world, do you submit to** [obey] **its rules: 'Do not handle! Do not taste! Do not touch!'?** [Paul is speaking about so-called holy relics, holy objects, food offered to idols, superstitions, and meaningless traditions which both Gentiles and the apologists observed.] **These rules** [foolish notions], **which have to do with things that are all destined to perish with use, are based on merely human commands and teachings."**

Colossians 2:23: "Such regulations indeed have an appearance of wisdom, with their self-imposed worship, their false humility and their harsh treatment of the body, but they lack any value in restraining sensual indulgence."

Colossians Chapter 3

Colossians 3:1-3: "Since, then, you have been raised [from the dead, spiritually speaking] **with Christ, set your hearts on things above, where Christ is, seated at the right hand of God. Set your minds on things above, not on earthly things. For you died, and your life** [of sin] **is now hidden with Christ[**'s righteousness] **in God."**

Colossians 3:4-6: "When Christ, who is your life, appears, then you also will appear with him in glory. Put to death, therefore, whatever belongs to your earthly nature: sexual immorality, impurity, lust, evil desires and greed, which is idolatry. Because of these, the wrath of God is coming."

Colossians 3:7-10: "You used to walk in these ways, in the life you once lived. But now you must also rid yourselves of all such things as these: anger, rage, malice, slander, and filthy language from your lips. Do not lie to each other, since you

have taken off your old self with its practices and have put on the new self, which is being renewed in knowledge in the image of its Creator."

Colossians 3:11-13: "Here there is no Gentile or Jew, circumcised or uncircumcised, barbarian, Scythian, slave or free, but Christ is all, and is in all. Therefore, as God's chosen people [notice in the previous sentence who constitutes God's chosen people], holy and dearly loved, clothe yourselves with compassion, kindness, humility, gentleness and patience. Bear with each other and forgive one another if any of you has a grievance against someone. Forgive as the Lord forgave you."

Colossians 3:14-17: "And over all these virtues put on love, which binds them all together in perfect unity. Let the peace of Christ rule in your hearts, since as members of one body you were called to peace. And be thankful. Let the message of Christ dwell among you richly as you teach and admonish one another with all wisdom through psalms, hymns, and songs from the Spirit, singing to God with gratitude in your hearts. And whatever you do, whether in word or deed, do it all in the name of the Lord Jesus, giving thanks to God the Father through him."

Colossians 3:18-24: "Wives, submit yourselves to your husbands, as is fitting in the Lord. Husbands, love your wives and do not be harsh with them. Children, obey your parents in everything, for this pleases the Lord. Fathers, do not embitter your children, or they will become discouraged. Slaves, obey your earthly masters in everything; and do it, not only when their eye is on you and to curry their favor, but with sincerity of heart and reverence for the Lord. Whatever you do, work at it with all your heart, as working for the Lord, not for human masters, since you know that you will receive an inheritance from the Lord as a reward. It is the Lord Christ you are serving."

Colossians 3:25: "Anyone who does wrong will be repaid for their wrongs, and there is no favoritism [in God's view]."

Colossians Chapter 4

Colossians 4:1-4: "Masters, provide your slaves with what is right and fair, because you know that you also have a Master in heaven. Devote yourselves to prayer, being watchful and thankful. And pray for us, too, that God may open a door for our message, so that we may proclaim the mystery of Christ, for which I am in chains. Pray that I may proclaim it clearly, as I should."

Colossians 4:5-6: "Be wise in the way you act toward outsiders; make the most of every opportunity. Let your conversation be always full of grace, seasoned with salt, so that you may know how to answer everyone."

Colossians 4:7-9: "Tychicus will tell you all the news about me. He is a dear brother, a faithful minister and fellow servant in the Lord. I am sending him to you for the express purpose that you may know about our circumstances and that he may encourage your hearts. He is coming with Onesimus, our faithful and dear brother, who is one of you. They will tell you everything that is happening here."

Colossians 4:10-11: "My fellow prisoner Aristarchus sends you his greetings, as does Mark, the cousin of Barnabas. (You have received instructions about him; if he comes to you, welcome him.) Jesus, who is called Justus, also sends greetings. These are the only Jews among my co-workers for the kingdom of God, and they have proved a comfort to me."

Colossians 4:12-13: "Epaphras, who is one of you and a servant of Christ Jesus, sends greetings. He is always wrestling in prayer for you, that you may stand firm in all the will of God, mature and fully assured. I vouch for him that he is working hard for you and for those at Laodicea and Hierapolis."

Colossians 4:14-16: "Our dear friend Luke, the doctor, and Demas send greetings. Give my greetings to the brothers and sisters at Laodicea, and to Nympha and the church in her house. After this letter has been read to you, see that it is also read in the church of the Laodiceans and that you in turn read the letter from Laodicea."

Colossians 4:17-18: "Tell Archippus: 'See to it that you complete the ministry you have received in the Lord.' I, Paul, write this greeting in my own hand. Remember my chains. Grace be with you."

Romans

Introduction

I hope you have carefully studied the previous three commentaries. It is easy to get lost in the forest of Paul's logic within the book of Romans unless you first understand the problems he faced and have a general idea how he intended to resolve them. Remember the five problems from the Galatians introduction that constantly dogged Paul's missionary efforts. For best results, refer to your favorite translation as you read.

The apostle Paul wrote the book of Romans about fifteen years before Rome destroyed Jerusalem in A.D. 70. One word of caution: Paul does not say one thing in one place and then say the opposite in another. Many people distort Paul's writings by making him appear to have meant something he did not intend. Peter wrote, **"Bear in mind that our Lord's patience means salvation, just as our dear brother Paul also wrote you with the wisdom that God gave him. He writes the same way in all his letters, speaking in them of these matters. His letters contain some things that are hard to understand, which ignorant and unstable people distort, as they do the other Scriptures, to their own destruction."**[1]

Therefore, to make sense of the book of Romans and avoid creating internal conflict within the Bible, we have to step back in time and enter into the local realities then facing the church. The church in Rome was sharply divided and about to implode due to ethnic, religious, and cultural warfare. Gentile and Jewish converts were at an impasse and no one could resolve a basket full of conflicts that confronted the early church. Even though Paul had not been to Rome, he was compelled by the Holy Spirit to "wade in" and this is why he wrote the book of Romans. It is believed that Paul wrote the epistle while in Corinth.

---

1   2 Peter 3:15-16

The setting is about 25 years after the feast at Pentecost recorded in Acts 2. According to the Bible, some Jews from Rome attended the feast in Jerusalem[1] and were converted to Christianity. Jewish converts took the gospel of Jesus (or what they knew of it) back to Rome and a church sprang up. The situation for Christians in Rome was very difficult because there was a prevailing hatred for Jews throughout the Roman government. Any association with Jews was an invitation for ridicule, hatred, and persecution. The Romans considered Christians a sect of Jews (Jesus was a Jew), so Jews and Christians were treated with the same contempt. Anti-Semitism caused Gentile converts to cautiously keep themselves from anything or anyone who looked Jewish. As a well-traveled Roman citizen and Jew, Paul knew that if the hostilities continued within the church at Rome, Christianity could be separated from its Jewish foundation, the gospel of Jesus could become corrupted, and the overall effect on Christianity would become toxic.

As you read Paul's letter to the Romans, notice that his tone changes from time to time; and be alert for the following issues because he mentions them often:

1. *Obedience* about 20 times
2. *Faith* about 40 times
3. *Righteousness* about 30 times
4. *Law* about 70 times
5. *Sin* about 50 times
6. *Grace* about 20 times
7. *The Spirit* about 35 times

Romans Chapter 1

Paul had not visited Rome when he wrote this letter to the church in Rome, but he knew and was known by some of the Christians living there. He introduced himself to the church as a servant of Jesus Christ, a man set apart to deliver "the gospel of God." After a brief introduction, he addresses the great wickedness of the pagans in

---

1 Acts 2:5-11

Rome. He highlights the depravity of the pagans so that in Chapter 2, he can forcefully chastise Gentile believers who are doing the very same things. (Perhaps you have heard it said, "As the world goes, so goes the church – only a little slower.") Notice also, as you read Chapter 1, that Paul keeps inserting the Jews into his comments because "the gospel of God" cannot be separated from Abraham and the history of the Jews. In fact, Jesus is a descendant of King David!

Romans 1:1-4: "**Paul, a servant of Christ Jesus, called to be an apostle and set apart for the gospel of God—the gospel he promised beforehand through his prophets in the Holy Scriptures regarding his Son, who as to his earthly life was a descendant of David, and who through the Spirit of holiness was appointed the Son of God in power by his resurrection from the dead: Jesus Christ our Lord.**"

Romans 1:5-6: "**Through him** [Jesus] **we received grace and apostleship to call all the Gentiles to the obedience that comes from faith for his name's sake.** [Paul describes his mission as calling people from among the Gentiles to obedience, but what law are the "called" supposed to obey? What acts of obedience stem from faith?] **And you** [already in the church] **also are among those Gentiles who are called to** [obedience through faith because you] **belong to Jesus Christ.**"

Romans 1:7-8: "**To all in Rome who are loved by God and called to be his holy people: Grace and peace to you from God our Father and from the Lord Jesus Christ. First, I thank my God through Jesus Christ for all of you, because your faith is being reported all over the world.**"

Romans 1:9-12: "**God, whom I serve in my spirit in preaching the gospel of his Son, is my witness how constantly I remember you in my prayers at all times; and I pray that now at last by God's will the way may be opened for me to come to you.** [I have been in Corinth for a while and] **I long to see you so that I may impart to you some spiritual gift to make you strong—that is, that you and I may be mutually encouraged by each other's faith.**"

Romans 1:13-15: "I do not want you to be unaware, brothers and sisters, that I planned many times to come to you (but have been prevented from doing so until now) in order that I might have a harvest among you, just as I have had among the other Gentiles. I am obligated both to Greeks and non-Greeks, both to the wise and the foolish. That is why I am so eager to preach the gospel also to you who are in Rome."

Romans 1:16-17: "For I am not ashamed of the gospel, [unlike some of you in Rome,] because it is the power of God that brings salvation to everyone who believes: first to the Jew [the people through whom salvation came], then to the Gentile [who are now accepted as brothers]. For in the gospel the righteousness of God is revealed—a righteousness that is [granted to those who live] by faith from first to last [that is, everyone who obeys the Spirit though faith is given this righteousness], just as it is written: 'The righteous will live by faith.'"

Romans 1:18-20: "The wrath of God is being revealed from heaven [through visions and revelations given to the apostles, the coming wrath of God and the end of the world is better understood. Jesus will soon rise up] against all the godlessness and wickedness of people, who suppress the truth by their wickedness, since what may be known about God is plain to them, because God has made it plain to them. For since the creation of the world God's invisible qualities—his eternal power and divine nature—have been clearly seen, being understood from what has been made, so that people are without excuse."

Romans 1:21-23: "For although they knew [about] God['s actions in the past, like Noah's flood, Sodom and Gomorrah, and the rise and fall of empires], they neither glorified him as God nor gave thanks to him, but their thinking became futile and their foolish hearts were darkened. Although they claimed to be wise, they became fools and exchanged the glory of the immortal God for images made to look like a mortal human being and birds and animals and reptiles."

Romans 1:24-25: "**Therefore God gave them over** [as freewill beings, He gave them freedom to do as they choose] **in the sinful desires of their hearts to sexual impurity for the degrading of their bodies with one another. They exchanged the truth about God for a lie, and worshiped and served created things rather than the Creator—who is forever praised. Amen.**"

Romans 1:26-27: "**Because of this, God gave them over to shameful lusts. Even their women exchanged natural sexual relations for unnatural ones. In the same way the men also abandoned natural relations with women and were inflamed with lust for one another. Men committed shameful acts with other men, and received in themselves the due penalty for their error** [which will be imposed on the guilty at the end of sin's drama]."

Romans 1:28-32: "**Furthermore, just as they did not think it worthwhile to retain the knowledge of God, so God gave** [allowed] **them over to a depraved mind, so that they do what ought not to be done. They have become filled with every kind of wickedness, evil, greed and depravity. They are full of envy, murder, strife, deceit and malice. They are gossips, slanderers, God-haters, insolent, arrogant and boastful; they invent ways of doing evil; they disobey their parents; they have no understanding, no fidelity, no love, no mercy. Although they know God's righteous decree that those who do such things deserve death, they not only continue to do these very things but also approve of those who practice them.** [This is the result of turning away from God's law and the obedience that comes through faith. Many Christians are no different from the pagans. They practice gossip, commit slander, are sexually immoral, insolent, arrogant, boastful, senseless, faithless, heartless, and ruthless. Fools may think there is no God who takes notice of our behavior, but what will they say when they face the wrath of a righteous and holy God?**]**"

Romans Chapter 2

Paul opens this chapter chastising Jewish and Gentile converts for doing evil and for being critical and judgmental. Then, he surprises both groups with his comments that a genuine Jew is not what the Gentiles think or what most Jews practice. Paul disarms their ethnic conflict by explaining why both parties are wrong. Paul also addresses a nagging question that both parties wrestled with: How are people saved before Jesus' birth when there was no gospel, and how are people saved after the cross even though they do not have any knowledge of Jesus or His gospel?

Romans 2:1-2: "[As an apostle called by the Lord, I must rebuke the righteous facade that many of you in Rome wear.] **You, therefore, have no excuse, you** [sit in judgment, those of you] **who pass judgment on someone else, for at whatever point you judge another, you are condemning yourself, because you who pass judgment do the same things. Now we know that God's judgment** [condemnation is] **against those who do such things is based on truth.**"

Romans 2:3-5: "**So when you, a mere human being, pass judgment on them** [others] **and yet do the same things, do you think you will escape God's judgment? Or do you show contempt for the riches of his kindness, forbearance and patience, not realizing that God's kindness** [should] **is intended to lead you to repentance? But because of your stubbornness and your unrepentant heart, you are storing up wrath against yourself for the day of God's wrath, when his righteous judgment will be revealed.**"

Romans 2:6-8: "[Dear brothers and sisters, let me be clear, Scripture teaches that:] **God 'will repay each person according to what they have done.'** [Did you notice the phrase, 'according to what they have done?' The brother of Jesus wrote, *"You see that a person is considered righteous by what they do and not by faith alone."*[1] Both men are saying that our knowledge of God's will should determine

---

1   James 2:24, italics mine

our words and actions.] **To those who by persistence** [yes, it is a struggle to live by faith] **in doing good seek glory, honor and immortality, he will give eternal life. But for those who are self-seeking and who reject the truth and follow evil, there will be wrath and anger** [at the end of the age]."

Romans 2:9-11: "**There will** [come a time when there will] **be trouble and distress for every human being who does evil: first for the Jew** [because he was first to know God's will and had an opportunity to do good], **then for the Gentile; but glory, honor and peace** [will be awarded] **for everyone who does good: first for the Jew** [those who embraced the gospel of God and did good], **then for the Gentile. For God does not show favoritism**[; He loves and treats Jews and Gentiles the same]."

Romans 2:12-13: "[Consider God's fairness for those who have not heard the gospel of God.] **All who sin apart from the law** [that is, sinned having no knowledge of God's law] **will also perish apart from the law** [this means, God's law will not be used to condemn them. God will judge these people according to their knowledge of right and wrong and their response to the Holy Spirit], **and all who sin under the law** [that is, had knowledge of God's law] **will be judged by the law. For it is not those who hear the law who are righteous in God's sight, but it is those who obey the law** [through faith, I am speaking of the Ten Commandments and the two laws of love,] **who will be declared righteous.**"

Romans 2:14-16: "**(Indeed, when Gentiles** [such as Pagans, Catholics, Hindus, Muslims, Protestants, and Atheists], **who do not have** [knowledge of] **the law, do by nature things required by the law, they are a law for themselves, even though they do not have** [knowledge of] **the law. They show** [by their actions] **that the requirements of the law are written on their hearts, their consciences also bearing witness** [that is, they feel no guilt because they obeyed whatever the Spirit – who speaks to every heart, commanded], **and** [if they are unsure about a matter, that is] **their thoughts sometimes accusing them and at other**

times [the Spirit is] **even defending them** [because He knows their obedience came through faith]**.) This** [revelation] **will take place on the day when God judges people's secrets through Jesus Christ, as my gospel declares."**

Romans 2:17-21: "Now you, if you call yourself a Jew; if you rely on [observing] **the law** [for justification] **and boast in God; if you know his will and approve of what is superior because you are instructed by the law; if you are convinced that you are a guide for the blind, a light for those who are in the dark, an instructor of the foolish, a teacher of little children, because you have in the law the embodiment of knowledge and truth—you, then, who teach others,** [why] **do you not teach yourself? You who preach against stealing, do you** [break the eighth commandment and] **steal?"**

Romans 2:22-24: "You who say that people should not commit adultery, do you [break the seventh commandment and] **commit adultery? You who abhor idols** [per the second commandment]**, do you rob temples** [by stealing the offerings left in front of the idols]**? You who boast in** [your knowledge of] **the law, do you dishonor God by breaking the law?** [Shame on you! You are a lying hypocrite!] **As it is written: 'God's name is blasphemed among the Gentiles because of you.'"**[1]

Romans 2:25-26: "[Consider both sides of this argument for a moment:] **Circumcision has value if you observe the law** [of Moses]**, but if you break** [even one point in] **the** [Levitical] **law, you have become as though you had not been circumcised** [because *"For whoever keeps the whole law and yet stumbles at just one point is guilty of breaking all of it."*[2]]**. So then, if those who are not circumcised keep** [God's law – the Ten Commandments and the two laws of love upon which the Ten Commandments are based – which say nothing about circumcision, if they fulfill] **the law's requirements, will they not be regarded** [by God as

---

1   Ezekiel 20:14; 36:22-23
2   James 2:10, italics mine

righteous through faith] **as though they were circumcised?** [In other words, obeying the Holy Spirit produces the same faith whether or not a person has knowledge of the law. You may think faith eliminates the law. On the contrary, faith magnifies God's law. *"The law of the Lord is perfect, refreshing the soul. The statutes of the Lord are trustworthy, making wise the simple. The precepts of the Lord are right, giving joy to the heart. The commands of the Lord are radiant, giving light to the eyes. The fear of the Lord is pure, enduring forever. The decrees of the Lord are firm, and all of them are righteous. They are more precious than gold, than much pure gold; they are sweeter than honey, than honey from the honeycomb."*[1]]"

Romans 2:27-29: "The one who is not circumcised physically and yet obeys the law [the Ten Commandments and the two laws of love] **will condemn you** [Jewish converts] **who, even though you have the written** [Levitical] **code and circumcision,** [and] **are a lawbreaker.** [In God's sight] **A person is not a Jew who is one only outwardly, nor is circumcision merely outward and physical. No, a person is a Jew who is one inwardly; and circumcision is circumcision of the heart, by the Spirit, not by the written code. Such a person's praise is not from other people, but from God."**

Romans Chapter 3

After explaining that salvation is based on a spiritual transformation, Paul discusses the identity of a true Jew. Paul asserts that being a genuine Jew is not a matter of ethnicity, religion, or culture. Furthermore, as he said in Chapter 2, God will deal fairly with those who know His law and those who do not. In this chapter, Paul addresses converts who thought obeying the Ten Commandments and the laws of Moses were required for salvation. He also addresses Gentile converts who were not convinced that sanctification was required.

Consider Paul's counsel: One day, a rich young man asked Jesus what he needed to do to have eternal life. Jesus replied, **"'If you**

---

1   Psalms 19:7-10, italics mine

want to enter life, keep the commandments.' 'Which ones?'
he inquired. Jesus replied, 'You shall not murder, you shall
not commit adultery, you shall not steal, you shall not give
false testimony, honor your father and mother, and love your
neighbor as yourself.' 'All these I have kept,' the young man
said. 'What do I still lack?' Jesus answered, 'If you want to be
perfect, go, sell your possessions and give to the poor, and you
will have treasure in heaven. Then come, follow me.' When the
young man heard this, he went away sad, because he had great
wealth. Then Jesus said to his disciples, 'Truly I tell you, it is
hard for someone who is rich to enter the kingdom of heaven.
Again I tell you, it is easier for a camel to go through the eye of
a needle than for someone who is rich to enter the kingdom of
God.'"[1]

The "eye of a needle" was a common phrase in Bible times describing
a tiny door built into the thick walls of ancient cities. The door was
barely large enough for an adult to pass through. Its purpose was
safety, not only for the city, but also for weary travelers arriving
after dark. A traveler could enter the city for refuge, but his livestock
had to remain tethered outside.

This story illustrates elements about faith you need to know before
reading Chapter 3. Jesus did not confront the young man with the first
four commandments because the young man was fully convinced he
loved God appropriately. Jesus gently confronted the rich young man
with the last six commandments because Jesus wanted the young
man to examine and see for himself that he was deficient. When
we *fulfill* the Ten Commandments, they sanctify us. The young man
responded that he had kept the commandments, but *observing* the
law and *fulfilling* the law are very different experiences. Knowing
the young man was spiritually blind, Jesus opened his eyes to his
true condition by challenging the young man to *fulfill* the second
law of love by selling everything he owned, giving up the money
and following Him. Jesus framed His response to demonstrate that

---

1   Matthew 19:17-24

love and faith are necessary to *fulfill* the Ten Commandments! Jesus offered the young man the incredible opportunity to be His disciple. What an honor to be a companion of the Creator of the universe, the Savior of the world, the self-existing "I AM" and yet, the young man turned away. Spiritual blindness is such a curse.[1]

Living by faith is contrary to human nature and this is why living by faith requires a new heart. Our spiritual nature must reign over our sinful nature to live by faith. The rich young man's sinful nature was offended by Jesus. His wealth gave him respect in the community, wealth enabled him to have servants and they did whatever he wanted, wealth permitted him to buy whatever he wanted and to go wherever he wanted. The reason anyone would forfeit the power and privilege that comes with wealth is because the Holy Spirit has transformed them. Born-again people are transformed by the Holy Spirit. They see the treasurers of this world are tinsel and spiritual things are valuable and essential. Souls are more valuable than savings. Love for God and neighbor produces greater joy than leisure. The fruit of the indwelling Spirit is far more satisfying than an insatiable appetite for the pleasures of sin. However, this transformation of values is only possible through the miracle of rebirth.

Paul teaches in this chapter that what matters most to God is whether or not a person will obey the voice of the Holy Spirit because God speaks to each of us through Him. The rich young ruler heard from God and his faith was tested. For Jewish converts in Rome, Paul proves that keeping the law cannot merit salvation (remember the rich young ruler). For Gentile converts, Paul proves the law of God cannot be separated from living by faith. Understanding both arguments so that Paul's writing is not put into a state of internal conflict takes some effort. One last point, since the Gentiles in Rome wanted to distance themselves from the Jews for ethnic and cultural reasons, Paul inserts the role of Jews into this chapter because the law of God came through the Jews!

---

1   Revelation 3:14-22

Romans 3:1-2: "[Contrary to what the Roman government officials say, I am not ashamed of being a Jew. I am a Jew, but not as they understand a Jew. The Father has created a new Israel through Christ who is the eternal King of the Jews. God had to do this because of His unilateral promises made to Abraham. When it became clear that biological Israel failed, God raised up a 'self-selecting' Israel made up of those who wanted to obey the Holy Spirit! In God's sight, all born-again believers in Christ are the offspring of Abraham. To understand this phenomenon,] **What advantage, then, is there in being a** [biological] **Jew, or what value is there in circumcision? Much in every way! First of all, the Jews** [biological descendants of Abraham] **have been entrusted with the very words of God.**"

As Paul just said, "a man is a Jew if he is one inwardly; and circumcision is circumcision of the heart, by the Spirit, not by written code." Therefore, anyone who has a circumcised heart is a spiritual Jew and a member of 'New Covenant Israel.'[1]

Romans 3:3-6: "What if some [Jews] **were unfaithful? Will their unfaithfulness nullify God's faithfulness? Not at all!** [God's promises to Abraham have not been nullified by our unfaithfulness as a people.] **Let God be true, and every human being a liar. As it is written: 'So that you** [O Lord] **may be proved right when you speak and prevail when you judge.' But if our unrighteousness** [as biological descendants of Abraham] **brings out God's righteousness more clearly** [by abolishing the Levitical code and throwing open the doors to the Gentiles[2] through His Son's death and resurrection]**, what shall we say? That God is unjust in bringing his wrath on us** [the nation of Israel]**? (I am using a human argument.) Certainly not! If that were so, how could God judge the world** [remember, He shows no favoritism]**?**"

---

1   For further information, see wake-up.org/pauls-conversion-information
2   Ephesians 2

Romans 3:7-8: "**Someone might** [twist my words and foolishly] **argue, 'If my falsehood enhances God's truthfulness and so increases his glory, why am I still condemned as a sinner?'** [This is evil and foolish thinking.] **Why not say—as some** [Jewish apologists] **slanderously claim that we say—'Let us do evil that good may result'?** [Regarding them, I say,] **Their condemnation is just!**"

Romans 3:9-18: "**What shall we conclude then? Do we** [biological Jews] **have any advantage** [over the Gentiles]? **Not at all! For we have already made the charge that Jews and Gentiles alike are all under the power of sin. As it is written** [of mankind in Psalms and Isaiah]: **'There is no one righteous, not even one; there is no one who understands; there is no one who seeks God. All have turned away, they have together become worthless; there is no one who does good, not even one.'**[1] **'Their throats are open graves; their tongues practice deceit.'**[2] **'The poison of vipers is on their lips.'**[3] **'Their mouths are full of cursing and bitterness.'**[4] **'Their feet are swift to shed blood; ruin and misery mark their ways, and the way of peace they do not know.'**[5] **'There is no fear of God before their eyes.'**[6]"

Romans 3:19-20: "**Now we know that whatever the law** [the Ten Commandments and the two laws of love] **says, it says to those who are under the law, so that every mouth may be silenced and the whole world** [is] **held accountable to God. Therefore no one** [can be or] **will be declared righteous in God's sight by the works of the law; rather, through the law we become conscious of our sin.** [The law defines sin. This is its purpose.]"

Romans 3:21-24: "[Knowing that no one can be declared righteous in His sight, the Father sent Jesus to Earth to face temptations

1   Psalm 53:1-3
2   Psalm 5:9
3   Psalm 140:3
4   Psalm 10:7
5   Isaiah 59:7-8
6   Psalm 36:1

beyond any that human beings could face. Jesus overcame every temptation without sinning and thus created the righteousness sinners need for salvation. The Father will transfer the flawless life (the righteousness) of Jesus to any repentant sinner who will *fulfill* His laws of love through faith. This is the gospel of God:] **But now apart from** [observing] **the law the righteousness of God has been made known, to which the Law and the Prophets** [Old Testament] **testify. This righteousness is given through faith in Jesus Christ to all who believe. There is no difference between Jew and Gentile, for all have sinned and fall short of the glory of God, and all** [repentant sinners who live by faith] **are justified freely by his grace through the redemption that came by Christ Jesus."**

Romans 3:25-26: **"God presented** [Jesus] **Christ as a sacrifice of atonement,** [so that salvation was possible] **through the shedding of his blood—to be received by faith. He** [the Father] **did this to demonstrate his righteousness** [that is, the Father would not impose the second death on sinners before Jesus experienced the second death], **because in his forbearance he** [the Father] **had left the sins committed beforehand unpunished** [that is, Adam and Eve were not slain on the day they ate the forbidden fruit and no one has yet experienced the second death (except Jesus). The second death will be imposed on the wicked at the end of the 1,000 years[1]—**he** [the Father] **did it** [sent Jesus to the cross] **to demonstrate his righteousness at the present time, so as to be just** [fair] **and the one who justifies those who have faith in Jesus."**

Romans 3:27-28: **"Where, then, is** [any justification for] **boasting** [that I am a Jew, a member of the chosen race, a biological descendant of Abraham]**? It is** [now] **excluded. Because of what law? The law that requires works? No** [for no one has perfectly kept the law but Jesus, so there is no reason to boast about being a biological descendant of Abraham because salvation is not

---

1   Revelation 20:14

awarded on heritage or observing the law], **because of the law that requires faith. For we maintain that a person is justified by faith apart from the works of the law.** [In other words, a man is justified in God's sight when he obeys the Spirit, he goes, becomes and does (go-be-do) whatever the Holy Spirit tells him to do. Growth in salvific faith (the faith that leads to salvation) occurs in steps that have increasing rewards and consequences. We can be sure that Abraham's first test of faith was not the call to leave home and family behind, nor was Noah's first test of faith a call to build the ark. The Holy Spirit grows us in steps of faith because a man is justified by his continued faith. I am not saying that the law is nullified by faith, on the contrary, fulfilling the intent of the law requires incredible faith as you will shortly see!]"

Romans 3:29-31: "[Will God save pagans who knew nothing of His law? Yes, of course, Paul has already explained this.] **Or is God the God of Jews only? Is he not the God of Gentiles too? Yes, of Gentiles too, since there is only one God, who will justify the circumcised** [who lived] **by faith and the uncircumcised** [who also live] **through that same faith. Do we, then, nullify the law by this faith? Not at all! Rather, we uphold the law.** [Keep reading, I will explain how.]"

Romans Chapter 4

Paul explains in Chapter 4 why Abraham is called the father of all who live by faith, whether Jew or Gentile, circumcised or uncircumcised. Paul first undermines the exclusivity which the Jews attributed to biological heritage. Second, he eliminates each excuse the Gentiles offered to disassociate from the Jews – the gospel of God comes through the Jews. Third, Paul makes the point that salvation is not based on perfect obedience. Abraham lied about his wife and later committed adultery with Hagar; and King David committed adultery and murder—yet both men believed God and lived by faith most of the time. Each paid dearly for his sins but neither man was defiant; each man lived by faith and their sins were atoned for.

Romans 4:1-3: "What then shall we say that Abraham, our forefather according to the flesh, discovered in this matter? If, in fact, Abraham was justified by works, he** [may have] **had something to boast about—but not before God.** [We know that Abraham lied to Pharaoh about Sarah being his sister.[1] Therefore, our forefather could not be justified through obedience, but] **What does Scripture say? 'Abraham believed God** [when God said He would make childless Abraham to have descendants as numerous as the stars], **and it was credited to him as righteousness.'"**[2]

Romans 4:4-8: "Now to the one who works, wages are not credited as a gift but as an obligation. However, to the one who does not work but trusts God who justifies the ungodly** [that is, repentant sinners], **their faith is credited as righteousness. David** [who committed adultery with Bathsheba and had her husband Uriah, one of his best friends, killed so no one would know about his deeds] **says the same thing when he speaks of the blessedness of the one to whom God credits righteousness apart from works: 'Blessed are those whose transgressions are forgiven, whose sins are covered. Blessed is the one whose sin the Lord will never count against them.'"**[3]

Romans 4:9-10: "Is this blessedness** [righteousness by faith] **only for the circumcised, or also for the uncircumcised? We have been saying that Abraham's faith was credited to him as righteousness. Under what circumstances was it credited? Was it after he was circumcised, or before? It was not after, but before!"**

Romans 4:11-12: "And he received circumcision as a sign, a seal** [a token in his flesh] **of the righteousness that he had by faith while he was still uncircumcised. So then, he is the father of all who believe but have not been circumcised, in order that righteousness might be credited to them. And he is then also**

---

1   Genesis 12:13
2   Genesis 15:6
3   Psalm 32:1-2

the father of the circumcised who not only are circumcised but who also follow in the footsteps of the faith that our father Abraham had before he was circumcised."

Romans 4:13-15: "**It was not through the law that Abraham and his offspring received the promise that he would be heir of the world, but** [he became the heir] **through the righteousness that comes by faith. For if those who depend on the law are heirs, faith means nothing and the promise is worthless, because** [all have sinned and we know the violation of] **the law brings wrath** [death]**. And where there is no law there is no transgression** [and no wrath]**.**"

Romans 4:16: "**Therefore, the promise** [of inheriting the promised land also] **comes by faith, so that it may be by grace and may be guaranteed to all Abraham's offspring—not only to those** [Gentiles] **who are of the law but also to those who have the faith of Abraham. He is the father of us all** [who live by faith]**.**"

Romans 4:17-21: "**As it is written: 'I have made you a father of many nations** [meaning not only the nation of Israel]**.' He is our father** [example] **in the sight of God, in whom he believed— the God who gives life to the dead and calls into being things that were not. Against all hope, Abraham in hope believed and so became the father of many nations, just as it had been said to him, 'So shall your offspring be.' Without weakening in his faith, he faced the fact that his body was as good as dead—since he was about a hundred years old—and that Sarah's womb was also dead. Yet he did not waver through unbelief** [for awhile] **regarding the promise of God, but was strengthened in his faith and gave glory to God, being fully persuaded that God had power to do what he had promised.**"

Romans 4:22-25: "**This is why 'it was credited to him as righteousness.' The words 'it was credited to him' were written not for him alone, but also for us, to whom God will credit** [the] **righteousness** [of Christ]**—for us who believe**

in him who raised Jesus our Lord from the dead. He was
delivered over to death for our sins and was raised to life for
our justification."

Romans Chapter 5

Paul explains a mystery in Chapter 5. When Adam sinned, he lost
his sinless nature and the curse of sin became hereditary. Therefore,
all of Adam's offspring have sinful natures. How does God save
people who have sinful natures? In preparation for this problem,
the Father ordained that salvation would be made available to all
repentant sinners who live by faith. A sinner becomes a repentant
sinner through the miracle of rebirth: a born-again person forsakes
his sins and seeks to know and please God by following the Spirit
into a life of faith.

Paul explains in this chapter that before sin began, the Father
ordained that He would save repentant sinners through the transfer[1]
of their guilt to the temple through His Son's blood and the transfer
of Christ's righteousness (Jesus' perfect life) to everyone who lived
by faith.[2]

**Romans 5:1-2: "Therefore, since we have been justified through
faith, we have peace with God** [and the assurance of salvation]
**through our Lord Jesus Christ, through whom we have
gained access by faith into this grace in which we now stand.
And we boast in the hope of the glory of God."**

Romans 5:3-5: "Not only so [not only do we rejoice in the assurance
of salvation through faith in Christ], **but we also glory in our
sufferings** [for the gospel of God – the ridicule and hatred
around us does not offend us], **because we know that suffering
produces perseverance; perseverance, character; and
character, hope. And hope does not put us to shame, because
God's love has been poured out into our hearts through the
Holy Spirit, who has been given to us."**

---

1   For further information, see *wake-up.org/pauls-conversion-information*
2   Romans 5:19

Romans 5:6-11: "You see, at just the right time [predicted in Daniel 9], **when we were still powerless** [uninformed and living in darkness], **Christ died for the ungodly** [all sinners]. **Very rarely will anyone die for a righteous person, though for a good person someone might possibly dare to die. But God demonstrates his own love for us in this: While we were still sinners, Christ died for us.** [In other words, the Father loved us before we could know or worship Him.] **Since we have now been justified by his** [Christ's] **blood, how much more shall we be saved from God's wrath** [the second death] **through him! For if, while we were God's enemies, we were reconciled to him through the death of his Son, how much more, having been reconciled, shall we be saved through** [the transfer of] **his** [perfect] **life** [that is, Christ's righteousness to our account]**! Not only is this so, but we also boast in God through our Lord Jesus Christ, through whom we have now received reconciliation** [as sons and daughters of God]."

Romans 5:12-15: "**Therefore, just as sin entered the world through one man, and death through sin, and in this way death came to all people, because all sinned—To be sure, sin** [the violation of law] **was in the world before the law was given** [at Mt. Sinai], **but sin is not charged against anyone's account where there is no** [knowledge of God's will or] **law. Nevertheless, death reigned from the time of Adam to the time of Moses** [proving that death comes upon the ignorant as well as the informed], **even over those who did not** [deliberately] **sin by breaking a command, as did Adam, who is a pattern of the one to come.** [Adam was a pattern of Christ in that Adam is the biological father of all mankind, and Abraham is called the father of the faithful, so Jesus, our Savior is called the Father of the redeemed.[1]] **But the gift** [of salvation] **is not like the trespass. For if the many died by the trespass of the one man** [because of the consequence of sin], **how much more did God's grace and the gift that came by the grace of the one man,**

---
1   See Isaiah 9:6.

Jesus Christ, overflow to the many [because of Christ's perfect life and death, every repentant sinner is assured of eternal life if he is willing to put his faith in Christ]**!"**

Romans 5:16-18: **"Nor can the gift of God be compared with the result of one man's sin: The judgment** [that] **followed** [Adam's] **one sin and brought condemnation, but the gift** [that] **followed** [on the cross, after] **many trespasses and brought justification. For if, by the trespass of the one man, death reigned through that one man** [death came upon all mankind through Adam], **how much more will those who receive God's abundant provision of grace and of the gift of righteousness reign in life through the one man, Jesus Christ! Consequently, just as one trespass resulted in condemnation for all people, so also one righteous act resulted in justification and life for all people** [who will live by faith].**"**

Romans 5:19: **"For just as through the disobedience of the one man the many were made sinners** [the curse of sin is genetic, passed down to each generation], **so also through the** [perfect] **obedience of the one man** [Jesus] **the many will be made righteous** [through faith].**"**

Romans 5:20-21: **"The law** [first five books of the Bible] **was brought in** [through Moses] **so that** [man's knowledge of right and wrong, good and evil, health and happiness could expand and as a result, our knowledge and awareness of sin's curse increased. This was done so that our understanding of] **the trespass** [the consequences of sin] **might increase. But** [in those places] **where** [the knowledge of] **sin increased,** [our knowledge of God's] **grace increased all the more, so that, just as sin reigned in death** [that is, sin brings death to everything – even if we sin through ignorance or defiance, death still comes], **so also** [God has opened our eyes and hearts that we might behold the knowledge of how His] **grace might reign through righteousness to bring** [us] **eternal life through Jesus Christ our Lord."**

Romans Chapter 6

After Paul explains justification by faith in the previous three chapters, he moves forward into sanctification in the next three chapters because, **"without holiness** [sanctification] **no one will see the Lord."**[1] I encourage you to read these three chapters in one sitting because sanctification is not optional. Sanctification is how fellowship with God becomes possible. It is the process of learning to love as God loves. The sanctification process prepares us to live in God's house.

While on Mt. Sinai, Moses said to the Lord, **"If you are pleased with me, teach me your ways so I may know you and continue to find favor with you."**[2] Sanctification is an eternal process. It consists of learning God's ways and assimilating God's character of perfect love.

Many Christians minimize or ignore the sanctification part of the Christian life. It is as though justification is everything and sanctification is unimportant! Sure, getting something very valuable for free (justification) appeals to our greedy sinful nature, but our gracious and loving Father is deeply concerned about our preparation for life with the angels, Jesus, the Holy Spirit, and Himself.

Think about this: Even though they were created with sinless natures, the Father lost one-third of heaven's angels to rebellion. Therefore, the Father requires all repentant sinners undergo a preparation process for eternal life. Of course, repentant sinners, like the thief on the cross, who receive Jesus during the last moments of life, do not have much time for sanctification. This is not a problem. At the Second Coming, the thief will be resurrected and given a sinless nature[3] and his sanctification will continue in the same way as the sanctification of all of the saints! Each repentant sinner will continue to **"mature, attaining to the whole measure of the fullness of Christ."**[4] **"The righteous will flourish like a palm tree, they will**

---

1   Hebrews 12:14, insertion mine
2   Exodus 33:13
3   1 Corinthians 15:53
4   Ephesians 4:13

grow like a cedar of Lebanon; planted in the house of the Lord, they will flourish in the courts of our God."[1]

Sanctification requires faith through a three-step process: First, the Holy Spirit has to bring us to a place where we admit to God and ourselves that a certain behavior is a sin. Second, knowing that any cherished sin disconnects us from God's power, we have to confess "it is a sin" before we can be freed from it. Third, we then have to wrestle with our sinful nature, doing everything we can to overcome the sin. The struggle is exhausting and frustrating. After we prove to ourselves and God that we cannot achieve the victory we intensely want, our need of the Savior will become very real. Seeking victory through faith is difficult. Failure after failure is discouraging. Therefore, clinging to the promises of Jesus until He blesses us with the victory is what the school of sanctification through faith is all about.

Wrestling with God for victory is a divine privilege. This is what Jacob did just before he met Esau. After Jesus saw Jacob's remorse for his sin, Jesus blessed him and changed his name to Israel because of his faith and perseverance. Only born-again people want to stay within this bittersweet process. It is too difficult and distasteful for the sinful nature. Truancy from the school of sanctification explains fourteen centuries of repetitious failures by ancient Israel. There were far more "descendants of Jacob" than "descendants of Israel." Paul wrote, **"For not all who are descended from Israel are Israel."**[2]

Consider the life of Jesus, the "Author and Finisher of our faith": **"During the days of Jesus' life on earth, he offered up prayers and petitions with fervent cries and tears to the one who could save him from death, and he was heard because of his reverent submission** [even though He was not saved from death]. **Son though he was, he learned obedience from what he suffered and, once made perfect** [mature, a graduate from the school of sanctification],

---

1   Psalm 92:12-13
2   Romans 9:6

he became the source of eternal salvation for all who obey him [and are sanctified] and was designated by God to be high priest in the order of Melchizedek."[1]

You may be tempted to think that living by faith is not hard when compared to sanctification, but this perception immediately evaporates when you begin to live by faith. When God asks us to do something that is contrary to our sinful nature like avoiding retaliation against another or if God asks us to do something that comes with a significant price like to take a bold stand against evil, our faith is tested. The Holy Spirit may urge you to humble yourself and make restitution to someone you hurt, take an embarassing stand on a matter among your peers that is socially unacceptable, or simply share the gospel with someone who appears to be defiant. The Holy Spirit wants to use us to glorify Jesus, but we cannot glorify Him without faith. It takes determined faith to follow Jesus; remember the rich young man's sorrow when he chose not to exercise his faith. The Holy Spirit ensures the price for obedience is appropriate at all times. The rungs on the ladder of faith are not ten feet apart. When God asks the impossible, He makes the impossible possible, but you can be sure that whatever He asks will involve an uncomfortable stretch.

Romans 6:1-5: "[God's amazing grace has been extended to all sinners so that everyone can be justified through faith alone!] **What shall we say, then? Shall we go on sinning** [violating the law] **so that** [our need for] **grace may increase? By no means!** [When we received the gift of the Holy Spirit,] **We are those who have died to sin** [sin's attraction]; [so] **how can we live in it** [and be a part of it] **any longer? Or don't you know that all of us who were baptized into Christ Jesus were baptized into his death?** [When we chose to become a disciple of Jesus] **We** [died to the demands of the flesh and] **were therefore buried with him through baptism into** [His] **death in order that, just as Christ was raised from the dead through the glory of the Father, we too may** [leave our sinful thoughts, words,

---

1   Hebrews 5:7-10. For further study, see *wake-up.org/pauls-conversion-information*

and actions behind and] **live a new life** [through the indwelling power of the Holy Spirit]. **For if we have been united with him in a death like his, we will certainly also be united with him in a resurrection like his."**

Romans 6:6-7: "[This is the miracle of being born again: The Holy Spirit gives us an appetite and interest for spiritual things. The Spirit constantly seeks to draw us toward Jesus by pulling us away from the demands of the flesh.] **For we know that our old self was crucified with him** [when we surrendered to the call of the Spirit] **so that the body** [in which we live, that is naturally attracted to sin and] **ruled by sin might be done away with, that we should no longer be slaves to sin—because anyone who has died has** [no response to sin, He has] **been set free from sin** [sin's power through death]."

Romans 6:8-11: "**Now if we died with Christ** [if we allow the indwelling Holy Spirit to make us unresponsive to sin each day], **we believe that we will also live with him** [for eternity]. **For we know that since Christ was raised from the dead, he cannot die again; death no longer has mastery over him. The death he died, he died to sin once for all; but the life he lives, he lives to** [serve] **God** [the Father]. **In the same way, count yourselves dead to sin but alive to** [to serve] **God** [the Father] **in Christ Jesus."**

Romans 6:12-15: "**Therefore do not let sin reign** [have its way] **in your mortal body so that you obey its evil desires. Do not offer any part of yourself to sin** [guard your eyes, ears, hands, feet and mouth! Do not use them] **as an instrument of wickedness, but rather offer yourselves** [as servants] **to God as those who have been brought from death to life; and offer every part of yourself to him as an instrument of righteousness. For sin shall no longer be your master,** [if the Holy Spirit lives within you, He will set you free one day at a time] **because you are not under the law** [that is, your salvation is not based on perfect compliance with God's law – no one but Jesus has achieved the righteousness which the law demands], **but** [you are] **under grace.** [Be careful how you apply this because God has sufficient grace for repentant sinners, but no grace for defiant and rebellious law breakers.] **What then? Shall we sin** [ignore the law of God] **because we are not under the law but under grace? By no means!"**

Romans 6:16-18: **"Don't you know that when you offer yourselves to someone as obedient slaves, you are slaves of the one you obey**—[so ask yourself] **whether you are slaves to sin, which leads to death, or to obedience, which leads to righteousness? But thanks be to God that, though you used to be slaves to sin, you have come to obey** [the gospel of God] **from your heart the pattern of teaching that has now claimed your allegiance.** [Therefore,] **You have been set free from** [slavery to] **sin and** [through humility, patience and obedience] **have become slaves to righteousness."**

Romans 6:19-23: **"I am using an example from everyday life because of your human limitations. Just as you used to offer yourselves as slaves to impurity and to ever-increasing wickedness, so now** [you must] **offer yourselves as slaves to righteousness leading to holiness.** [And] **When you were slaves to sin, you were free from the control of righteousness. What benefit did you reap at that time from the things you are now ashamed of? Those things result in death! But now that you have been set free from sin and have become slaves of God, the benefit you reap leads to holiness** [your sanctification]**, and the result is eternal life. For the wages of sin** [violating God's law] **is death, but the gift of God is eternal life in Christ Jesus our Lord."**

Romans Chapter 7

Paul explains the function and role of God's law (the Ten Commandments) in this chapter. As a former Pharisee who was a legalistic zealot, he is in the best possible position to explain how faith works to the Jewish and Gentile converts in Rome. Paul explains a sanctification experience that occurred after he understood the intent of the tenth commandment since he had been a Christian for about 20 years when he wrote this chapter. Romans chapters 6-8 are tremendously encouraging when properly understood.

Romans 7:1-3: "[Because you now live to glorify God, there are three elements you must know about living the born-again experience which I will address in this chapter. First,] **Do you not know, brothers and sisters—for I am speaking to those who know the law**[of God]**—that the law has authority over someone only as long as that person lives? For example, by law a married woman is bound to her husband as long as he is alive, but if her husband dies, she is released from the law that binds her to him. So then, if she has sexual relations with another man while her husband is still alive, she is called an adulteress. But if her husband dies, she is released from that law** [of marriage] **and is not an adulteress if she marries another man.**"

Romans 7:4: "**So, my brothers and sisters,** [when you received Jesus as Lord and Master] **you also died to the law** [as a means to salvation] **through the body of Christ, that you might belong to another, to him who was raised from the dead, in order that we might bear fruit for God** [now that you have received Jesus as your Savior]."

Romans 7:5-6: "**For when we were in the realm of the flesh, the sinful passions** [which are natural and given little thought were suddenly] **aroused** [and made known] **by the law were at work in us** [and we didn't even realize it]**, so that we bore fruit for death. But now** [that we understand the boundaries between good and evil and]**, by dying to what once bound us, we have been released from the law** [the Ten Commandments as a means to salvation] **so that we serve** [God] **in the new way of the Spirit, and not in the old way of** [trying to establish our righteousness through] **the written code.**"

Romans 7:7-8: "**What shall we say, then? Is** [obeying] **the law sinful** [harmful, the wrong thing to do]**? Certainly not!**

Nevertheless, I would not have known what sin was had it not been for the law. For I would not have known what coveting really was if the law [tenth commandment] had not said, 'You shall not covet.' But [through the law my] sin [became known to me and], seizing [on] the opportunity [knowledge] afforded by the commandment, [it became clear to me that I actually coveted many things, so the law] produced in me [and revealed to me] every kind of coveting. For apart from the law, sin was dead. [Where there is no law, sin cannot be detected. This is why so many wish to do away with God's law, sin cannot be detected if there is no law!]"

Romans 7:9-12: "Once I was [very much] alive [zealously observing the law as a Pharisee and living quite happily, but I did not know I was living] apart from the law; but when the [Holy Spirit revealed the intent of God's] commandment [I] came [alive spiritually and then], sin sprang to life [I saw my guilt] and I died [was condemned to death]. I found that the very commandment that was intended to bring [abundant] life actually brought death. [I found that God forbids coveting because it leads to insatiable desires. If I am free of this sin, I have abundant joy. If I am controlled by covetousness, I am in bondage to unhappiness and death.] For sin [deadens our perceptions and heightens our passions, the curse of sin makes us unaware of the deeds and thoughts that lead to misery and sorrow. When the Holy Spirit opened my eyes to my true condition before God], seizing the opportunity afforded by the commandment, [I saw that my sinful nature had] deceived me, and [I quickly discovered that my sinful nature had to die. This highlights the purpose and role of God's law, it was] through the [tenth] commandment [that I realized my need to] put me [my sinful nature] to death. So then, [I confess] the law is holy, and the [tenth] commandment [forbidding covetous desires] is holy, righteous and good."

Romans 7:13-14: "Did that which is good [the commandment forbidding covetous desires], then, become death [useless] to me [when I accepted Jesus as my Savior]**? By no means! Nevertheless, in order that sin might be recognized as sin, it** [the law did what it is designed to do, it] **used what is good to bring about my death** [when I realized my covetous desires had to die in order to please God. Then, I discovered the second point about living the born-again life: The law declares what sin is]**, so that through the commandment sin might become utterly sinful.** [And] **We know that the law is spiritual; but I am** [naturally] **unspiritual, sold** [born] **as a slave to sin.** [Each person is born with a sinful nature because of the curse of sin. Until each person is awakened to his true condition before God, he is unaware of the priceless righteousness that comes through faith. I lived this way for many years, thinking my self-righteous actions were pleasing to God. Then I was shown my true condition on the road to Damascus. My zeal was self-centered and my religion was my god. When I saw God's sorrow with me, I was crushed and my self-righteousness evaporated. I realized my desperate need for the Savior.]"

Romans 7:15-19: "[I soon discovered that a born-again person has two warring natures. Consequently, I live with a constant struggle between my sinful nature and my spiritual nature. Regrettably, I still commit unintentional sins. One way to explain this phenomenon is this:] **I do not understand what I do. For what I want to do I do not do, but what I hate I do. And if I do what I do not want to do, I agree that the law is good.** [I admit that God's law is righteous.] **As it is,** [when I allow my sinful nature to spring to life] **it is no longer I myself who do it, but it is** [the curse of] **sin living in me. For I know that good itself does not dwell in me, that is, in my sinful nature. For I have the** [spiritual] **desire to do what is good, but I** [in my flesh] **cannot carry it out. For I do not do the good I want to do, but the evil I do not want to do—this I keep on doing.**"

Romans 7:20-25: "[And living as a born-again believer for 20 years, brings me to the third point:] **Now if I do what I do not want to do, it is no longer I who do it, but it is sin living in me**

that does it. So I find this law at work: **Although I want to do good, evil is right there with [in] me.** For in my inner being [in my spiritual nature] **I delight in God's law; but I [also] see another law at work in me, waging war against the law of my mind and** [body] **making me a prisoner of the law of sin at work within me. What a wretched man I am! Who will rescue me from this body that is subject to death? Thanks be to God, who delivers me through Jesus Christ our Lord! So then,** [until the sinful nature is removed] **I myself in my mind am a slave to God's law, but in my sinful nature a slave to the law of sin.** [There is a wonderful answer to Paul's question which was revealed to John after Paul's death. During the Great Tribulation, the sinful nature will be removed from all who will live by faith! The 144,000 will be sealed first.[1] As Martin Luther would later conclude, when a person is born again, the sinful nature remains, but it does not reign.]"

Romans Chapter 8

After explaining his born-again relationship with God's law, Paul continues his explanation on sanctification by writing a surprising statement! There is no condemnation for those who sin unintentionally! Some people maintain Romans 7 proves we are not responsible for our sins. This is not Paul's intent at all. His intent is to show that no matter how careful we are, the curse of sin within us will suddenly "pop out" and cause us to accidentally sin. We see Paul's intent stated in Hebrews: **"If we deliberately keep on sinning after we have received the knowledge of the truth, no sacrifice for sins is left, but only a fearful expectation of judgment and of raging fire that will consume the enemies of God."[2]** However, whenever we sin and are willing to confess it to our victim(s) and make restitution as needed, God is pleased!

Jesus said, **"Therefore, if you are offering your gift at the altar and there remember that your brother or sister has something**

---

1   For further study, see wake-up.org/pauls-conversion-information
2   Hebrews 10:26-27

against you, leave your gift there in front of the altar. First go and be reconciled to them; then come and offer your gift."[1] John wrote, "If we confess our sins [to those we have wronged and to God], he is faithful and just and will forgive us our sins and purify us from all unrighteousness. If we claim we have not sinned, we make him out to be a liar and his word is not in us."[2]

Romans 8:1-4: "[When I was thrown to the ground on the road to Damascus, Jesus appeared to me. Soon after, I received the gift of the Holy Spirit and repented of my horrible life and many sins. Since then, I have struggled with my sinful nature because I live to glorify the Father and my Savior, Jesus Christ. Of course, my efforts to be perfect in God's sight do not merit salvation. Instead, my efforts show that I am eager to please my God and my Savior. Even though I am far from perfect, I have the full assurance of salvation that comes through faith in Christ. I say this on the basis of God's grace; He has provided the righteousness that is needed for salvation through the perfect life of Jesus!

When He called me to preach the gospel of God to the Gentiles, I obeyed and the price has been minuscule when compared to the glory that is coming. My suffering for Jesus and His gospel has been nothing when compared to what He suffered for me. I want my life (thoughts, words, and actions) to honor and glorify Jesus and this is only possible through daily sanctification. As I said in the previous chapter, I cannot free myself from covetousness, but the Spirit can, by "deadening" my sinful nature! Until the Spirit removes my sinful nature, I am unhappy with myself, but joyful in the Lord. Let me further explain God's grace:] **Therefore, there is now no condemnation** [for unintentional sin in God's sight] **for those who are in Christ Jesus, because through Christ Jesus the law of the Spirit who gives life has set you free from the law of sin and death. For what the law** [tenth commandment condemning covetousness] **was powerless to do** [the commandment cannot change my heart] **because**

---

1   Matthew 5:23-24
2   1 John 1:9-10, insertion mine

it was weakened by the flesh [meaning I cannot escape the sinful nature that lives within me, therefore], **God did** [Himself established the righteousness that I need for salvation through Christ's perfect life and then He made it possible for my guilt to be transferred[1] to the temple altar in heaven] **by sending his own Son in the likeness of sinful flesh to be a sin offering** [He did this so that our guilt can be transferred to the temple through Jesus' innocent blood[2]]. **And so he condemned sin in the flesh** [God has made it clear that no sinner can save himself], **in order that the righteous requirement of the law might be fully met in us** [that is, the righteous requirements of the law have been met through Jesus and His righteousness is given to all], **who do not live according to the flesh but according to the Spirit."**

Romans 8:5-9: "Those who live according to the flesh have their minds set on what the flesh desires; but those who live in accordance with the Spirit have their minds set on what the Spirit desires. The mind governed by the flesh is death, but the mind governed by the Spirit is life and peace. The mind governed by the flesh is hostile to God; it does not submit to God's law, nor can it do so. Those who are in the realm of the flesh cannot please God. You, however, are not in the realm of the flesh but are in the realm of the Spirit, if indeed the Spirit of God lives in you [and we know that the Holy Spirit does not lead us away from God's law, but He leads us into fulfilling the law because God's law is righteous and holy. The Spirit wants to write God's law in our hearts and minds so that we can walk and live in perfect harmony with God]. **And if anyone does not have the Spirit of Christ, they do not belong to Christ."**

Romans 8:10-14: "But if Christ is in you, then even though your body is subject to death because of sin [your sinful nature is subdued], **the Spirit gives life because of righteousness** [that is, your sinful nature is under the dominion of your spiritual nature]. **And if the Spirit of him who raised Jesus from the**

1   For further study, see wake-up.org/pauls-conversion-information
2   Hebrews 8:1-5

dead is living in you, he who raised Christ from the dead will also give life to your mortal bodies because of his Spirit who lives in you. Therefore, brothers and sisters, we have an obligation—but it is not to the flesh, to live according to it. For if you live according to the flesh, you will die; but if by the Spirit you put to death the misdeeds of the body [this is the tug-of-war between the sinful nature and spiritual nature which I spoke about earlier], you will live. For those who are led by the Spirit of God are the children of God."

Romans 8:15-18: "The Spirit you received does not make you slaves, so that you live in fear again; rather, the Spirit you received brought about your adoption to sonship. And by him we cry, 'Abba, Father.' [Which means, our dear Father, the one who provides everything we need.] The Spirit himself testifies with our spirit [conscience] that we are God's children. Now if we are children [of God], then we are heirs—heirs of God and co-heirs with Christ, if indeed we share in his sufferings in order that we may also share in his glory. I consider that our present sufferings are not worth comparing with the glory that will be revealed in us."

Romans 8:19-23: "For the creation [those who live by faith] waits in eager expectation for the children of God to be revealed [glorified]. For the creation [in heaven] was subjected to frustration [by the rise of sin], not by its own choice, but by the will of the one who subjected it, [Adam. Because of the Father's love for the world, we rest] in hope that the creation itself will be liberated from its bondage to decay and brought into the freedom and glory of the children of God [just as promised]. We know that the whole creation [on Earth] has been groaning as in the pains of childbirth right up to the present time. Not only [is this] so [for the whole Earth], but we ourselves, who have the firstfruits of the Spirit, groan inwardly as we wait eagerly for our adoption to sonship, the redemption of our bodies."

Romans 8:24-28: "**For in this hope** [of redemption] **we were saved. But hope that is seen is no hope at all.** [*"Now faith is the substance of things hoped for."*[1]] **Who hopes for what they already have? But if we hope for what we do not yet have, we** [have to] **wait for it patiently. In the same way, the Spirit helps us in our weakness** [lack of patience and understanding]. **We do not know what we ought to pray for, but the Spirit himself** [knows our needs and He] **intercedes for us through wordless groans** [sounds]. **And he who searches our hearts knows the mind of the Spirit, because the Spirit intercedes for God's people in accordance with the will of God. And we know that in all things God works for the good of those who love him, who have been called according to his purpose."**[2]

Romans 8:29-32: "[Before the world was created, the Father intimately foreknew each of the 30+ billion people that would live on Earth. Therefore, He foreknew who would listen to Him through the voice of the Holy Spirit and who would not. (The Holy Spirit does not speak on His own.[3]) The Father predestined that each repentant sinner must participate in sanctification. As far as possible, He wants us restored into the likeness of Adam before his fall. Adam was made in the image of God. It is imperative that people understand that the Father predestined sanctification; He did not predestine who would be saved and who would not.] **For those God foreknew he also predestined to be conformed to the image of his Son, that he** [Jesus] **might be** [called] **the firstborn** [the preeminent] **among many brothers and sisters. And those he predestined, he also called; those he called, he also justified; those he justified, he also glorified** [through sanctification[4]]. **What, then, shall we say in response to these things? If God is for us, who can be against us? He who did not spare his own**

---

1   Hebrews 11:1 KJV, italics mine

2   For further study on predestination, see wake-up.org/pauls-conversion-information. Also, see Ephesians introduction.

3   John 16:13

4   John 17:17

Son, but gave him up for us all—how will he not also, along with him, graciously give us all things?"

Romans 8:33-36: "**Who will** [dare to] **bring any charge against those whom God has chosen? It is God who justifies. Who then is the one who condemns** [what God has justified]? **No one.** [Our salvation is assured because of] **Christ Jesus who died—more than that, who was raised to life—is at the right hand of God and is also interceding for us.** [So] **Who shall separate us from the love of Christ? Shall trouble or hardship or persecution or famine or nakedness or danger or sword? As it is written: 'For your sake we face death all day long; we are considered as sheep to be slaughtered.'"**

Romans 8:37-39: "**No, in all these things we are more than conquerors through him who loved us.** [Do not be discouraged or forfeit your hope of eternal life because of suffering and discouragement.] **For I am convinced that neither death nor life, neither angels nor demons, neither the present nor the future, nor any powers, neither height nor depth, nor anything else in all creation, will be able to separate us from the love of God that is in Christ Jesus our Lord.**"

Romans Chapter 9

Thus far, Paul's letter to the Romans can be broken down into three general segments: Chapters 1-2, Paul chastised the Gentile converts for behaving like the pagans and then condemning the pagans for doing the very same things. He also chastised the Jewish converts for being arrogant, legalistic, and aloof. To set the record straight, Paul declared that a Jew in God's sight, is a person whose heart has been circumcised by the Spirit. Chapters 3-5, Paul explained how God legitimately justifies everyone who lives by faith, both Jews and Gentiles. Chapters 6-8, Paul explained that God requires every believer in Jesus to undergo the sanctification process. Faith does not nullify God's law; the purpose of God's law is to define sin. The law can be understood in a secular (superficial) way and a spiritual (sanctifying) way! Each view is valid and important, but born-again believers are richly blessed after they experience the victory promised in God's covenant (freedom from slavery to sin).[1]

God's law constantly rebukes our sinful nature, as well as our faulty love for God and neighbor. Because the sinful nature remains within born-again people, Paul said there is no condemnation for those who unintentionally sin, but on the other hand, he also said there is no grace for those who continue to sin defiantly. This fact lays the groundwork for the next three chapters. The issue is this: From the time of Abraham, there have been two classes of his descendants. One class has maintained a state of defiance and the other class consists of repentant sinners, Jews and Gentiles, circumcised and uncircumcised, who live by faith.

Paul wrote, **"Nor because they are his descendants are they all Abraham's children. On the contrary, 'It is through Isaac that your offspring will be reckoned.'"**[2] The Jews said to Jesus, **" 'Abraham is our father,' they answered. 'If you were Abraham's children,' said Jesus, 'then you would do what Abraham did. As it is, you are looking for a way to kill me, a man who has told you the truth that I heard from God. Abraham did not do such things. You are doing the works of your own father.' 'We are not illegitimate children** [as you are]**,' they protested. 'The only Father we have is God Himself.'"**[3]

Romans 9:1-2: "I speak the truth in Christ—I am not lying, my conscience confirms it through the Holy Spirit— I have great sorrow and unceasing anguish in my heart [because Israel remains defiant]. [Here's why:]**"**

Romans 9:3-4: "For I could wish that I myself were cursed and cut off from Christ for the sake of my people, those of my own [Jewish] **race, the people of Israel.** [Consider the blessings which God promised to them if they would love Him and obey

---

1   John 8:34-36
2   Romans 9:7
3   John 8:39-41

Him. God chose the descendants of Abraham to be a kingdom of priests, the trustees of His gospel. He gave them many special blessings, such as:] **Theirs is the adoption of sonship** [through Abraham]**; theirs the** [possession of] **divine glory** [in the temple]**, the covenants** [given to Abraham and Moses]**, the receiving of the law** [the Ten Commandments written by God's own hand]**, the temple worship and the promises** [of becoming a kingdom of priests and kings]**."**

Romans 9:5-7: "Theirs are the patriarchs, and from them is traced the human ancestry of the Messiah, who is God over all, forever praised! Amen. It is not as though God's word had failed [even though Israel has failed]**. For not all who are descended from** [the loins of Jacob] **Israel are** [part of] **Israel. Nor because they are his descendants are they all Abraham's children. On the contrary** [Abraham fathered Ishmael, but God said]**, 'It is through Isaac that your offspring will be reckoned.'"**

Romans 9:8-9: "In other words, [God makes this perfectly clear,] **it is not the children by physical descent** [biological children] **who are God's children, but it is the children of the promise** [those who live by faith as did Abraham] **who are regarded as Abraham's offspring.** [*"'If you were Abraham's children,' said Jesus, 'then you would do what Abraham did.'"*[1]] **For this was how the promise was stated** [to Abraham]**: 'At the appointed time I will return** [to you]**, and Sarah will have a son.'"**

Romans 9:10-12: "Not only that [promise]**, but** [all of] **Rebekah's children were conceived at the same time by our father Isaac** [through whom God renewed the covenant which had been given to Abraham]**. Yet, before the twins** [Jacob and Esau] **were born or had done anything good or bad—in order that God's purpose in election might stand:** [God informed Rebekah that His plans would be carried out even though her firstborn son would grow up to despise his spiritual responsibilities. God told

---

1   John 8:39, italics mine

her of these matters to increase her faith because He is able to achieve His goals without violating the free will of any person. This is why the Scripture says] **not by** [human] **works but by** [faith in] **him who calls** [us]—[so] **she** [Rebekah] **was told** [in advance], **'The older will serve the younger.'"**

Romans 9:13: "Just as it is written: 'Jacob['s actions] **I loved, but Esau**['s actions] **I hated.'"**[1]

This did not mean God loved Isaac and hated Ishmael and Esau as persons. God loves every person equally![2] However, from the beginning of sin, God is executing His plan to save repentant sinners. This plan involves the selection and active participation of individuals whom God calls to serve as trustees of His gospel. God designed that some people would be chosen as trustees to carry the gospel to the rest of the people. He did this so the world could see what kind of wonderful and loving people the gospel of God creates. After Noah's flood, the descendants of Abraham were chosen as trustees (later called Jews). The beneficiaries of God's gospel were to be the Gentiles. Within the context of His plan, the statement, "Jacob I loved, but Esau I hated" means the following:

God wanted a child born to Abraham and Sarah *after* it was humanly impossible for them to have children. Abraham's firstborn was to be the heir of the covenant given to Abraham. But, after waiting for years on God, Abraham and Sarah lost faith in God. They justified Abraham's adultery with Hagar to produce a son. Ishmael, was born from the deeds of the flesh. Ishmael was born in sin (adultery) and God was dishonored. God's plan for "the promised son" was tarnished. Therefore, God not only hated the actions of Abraham and Sarah, He hated the results of their sin because their sin harmed Ishmael's life, Hagar's life and later on, Isaac's life.

Abraham's adultery frustrated God's plan to use Isaac as a figure of Jesus. Isaac was to be the "impossible" son born to Abraham and Sarah while Jesus would be the "impossible" son born of the virgin

---

1   Malachi 1:2-3
2   John 3:16; Acts 10:34

Mary. Isaac was to be the father of a nation of faith-full trustees as Jesus was to be the Father of the redeemed. Abraham had previously demonstrated that He was a man of great faith. This is why God chose Him to be the father of those who would live by faith!

Because living by faith is critical to God, God prevented Abraham and Sarah from having a child until Sarah was too old – to demonstrate that God's children are the result of a miracle, not the deeds of the flesh. Abraham and Sarah lost faith in God's promise and God hated their sin (not Ishmael). The moral of the story regarding the birth of Isaac and Jesus is this: Being born again is a miracle that cannot be achieved through human effort! No person can make himself born again, although many Christians are deceived by the idea that they can come to God and receive salvation whenever they want. **"Today, if you hear his voice, do not harden your hearts."**[1]

Later, when Esau and Jacob were about seventy years of age,* God hated the sin of Jacob and his mother when they conspired to steal the blessing that belonged to Esau (they resorted to the works of the flesh). Rebekah knew that Esau hated spiritual responsibilities and that Esau was not inclined toward serving God, and she desperately wanted Jacob (her favorite son) to have the blessing that rightfully belonged to Esau. Now, God had told her that Jacob would be the heir of the covenant before the boys were born so that she would not despair because of the realities she would observe for many years. Yet, she and Jacob failed to wait on the Lord, as did Abraham and Sarah, and Rebekah suffered for her sin. After she helped Jacob deceive Isaac, Because of Esau's threat, Jacob was forced to leave home and Rebekah never saw her favorite son again.

*Note: Jacob was about 70 years old when he deceived his father, Isaac. Here's the evidence: (a) Jacob was 130 years old when he moved into Egypt, (b) Joseph was 39 or 40 when his father moved into Egypt[2] and, (c) Joseph was born during Jacob's twentieth year with Laban.[3] Therefore, 130 minus 40 minus 20 equals 70.

---

1   Hebrews 3:7-8
2   Genesis 41:46,48; 45:4-6
3   Genesis 30:25; 31:38

When fleeing from Esau, Jacob confessed his sin and repented of his deed (and 20 years later, made full restitution to Esau). God reassured Jacob that He would bless Jacob with a vision of a ladder reaching from Earth to heaven. Years later, when Jacob returned to his homeland, God wrestled with Jacob to see if he was still sorry for deceiving his father and for cheating Esau out of the blessing due him as the firstborn. God was pleased with Jacob's response and He changed Jacob's name to Israel that night because Jacob was willing to wrestle with God, clinging to Him by a faith that would not let go.

After Jacob demonstrated his faith in God, God passed the covenant blessing from Isaac to Jacob. This reveals an interesting point in itself: Isaac wanted to pass the blessing to Esau, his favorite son, but God's covenant could not be passed along by man. Even though Esau was due to receive it, Esau refused to live by faith, so Rebekah and Jacob planned "to help God out." Esau was rejected on spiritual grounds; he could not serve as a trustee of the gospel. Thus, the phrase, "Jacob I loved, but Esau I hated" speaks of each man's qualification as a trustee of God's gospel. Through faith, humility, and repentance, Jacob became qualified as the next trustee of the covenant.

Romans 9:14-16: "What then shall we say? Is God unjust [because He only works with submissive people to accomplish His plan of salvation]**? Not at all! For he says to Moses, 'I will have mercy on whom I will have mercy, and I will have compassion on whom I will have compassion.'** [In other words, God declares, "I know what I am doing and what needs to be done, and I know who will cooperate with Me."] **It** [that is, one's acceptance or rejection for God's purposes] **does not, therefore, depend on human desire or effort, but on God's mercy** [choosing]**."**

Romans 9:17: "[We find in Scripture that God also works with defiant people to accomplish His purposes:] **For Scripture says to Pharaoh: 'I** [the Lord] **raised you up for this very purpose, that I might display my power in you** [through your obstinate rebellion] **and that my name might be proclaimed in all the earth.'"**

Romans 9:18: "Therefore God has mercy on whom he wants to have mercy [at times He chooses submissive people to accomplish His objectives], **and he hardens whom he wants to harden."**

He also chooses defiant people to accomplish His objectives. This does not indicate that God creates people with hard hearts or submissive hearts. Each person has a choice. When the carnal nature is confronted with God's authority, people will either respond by hardening their hearts or surrendering to the Holy Spirit. We discussed this in the previous chapter.[1] Therefore, when God confronted Pharaoh with a divine demand, the demand caused Pharaoh's arrogant, pompous, and selfish heart to become totally defiant. Pharaoh was arrogant and rebellious toward God's higher authority long before God gave the earthly ruler an ultimatum. God did not create Pharaoh to then destroy him. Instead God's demand aroused Pharaoh's selfish nature and his defiant response and subsequent destruction became legendary.

Romans 9:19-21: "One of you will say to me: 'Then why does God still blame us [for being rebellious]? **For who is able to resist his will?'** [In other words, one of you might say to me: Man has no choice. God made us what we are. Whether we are defiant like Pharaoh or submissive like Abraham, Isaac and Jacob, it makes no difference. God controls everything and everyone.] **But who are you, a human being, to talk back to God? 'Shall what is formed say to the one who formed it, "Why did you make me like this?" ' Does not the potter have the right to make out of the same lump of clay some pottery for special purposes and some for common use?** [God has a plan that is higher and larger than man can understand and His plans are carefully, thoughtfully, and deliberately designed in love to achieve the maximum amount of good.]"

Romans 9:22: "[Consider this reasoning for a moment:] **What if God, although choosing to show his wrath** [toward rebellious angels] **and** [at the same time to] **make his** [awesome] **power known** [to the

---

1   Romans 8:1-6

universe], [He] **bore with great patience** [their rebellion in heaven because He had larger matters to resolve first – even though they became] **the objects of his wrath—prepared for destruction?** [In other words, what if God bore with great patience the rebellion of our own forefathers even though later they became objects of His wrath and were ultimately destroyed in the wilderness?]"

Romans 9:23-24: "**What if he did this** [for the rebellious angels and our forefathers alike] **to make the riches of his glory known to** [submissive people, that is, believers in Christ] **the objects of his mercy, whom he prepared in advance** [that is, He foreknew us from the beginning] **for glory—even us** [the despised of Earth], **whom he also called** [out], **not only from the Jews but also from the Gentiles?**"

Paul uses God's lengthy patience with rebellious angels and Israel to drive home the point that when God is deliberately patient and longsuffering, He always has a glorious purpose for delaying His wrath. His actions are governed by love and wisdom. His purposes for being patient are timely, wonderful, grand, and far reaching. Paul brings up this point to say that the Father has been very patient with Israel even though He foreknew Israel's rebellion and rejection of Jesus, but the Father had a purpose for being patient with Israel's rebellion that is larger than Israel! His purpose is to save a huge number of Gentiles.

Romans 9:25-26: "[Do you remember the prophecies given to us in the Old Testament:] **As he says in Hosea**[1]: '**I will call them "my people"** [the Gentiles] **who are not my people; and I will call her "my loved one"** [the Gentiles] **who is not my loved one,' and,** [when God's kingdom is finally set up] '**In the very place where it was said to them, "You are not my people," there**[, this prediction will be fulfilled,] **they will be called "children of the living God."** [and these will be the descendants of Abraham, which will be more numerous than the stars in the sky or the dust of the ground!]' "

1　Hosea 2:23

Romans 9:27-29: "Isaiah[1] **cries out concerning Israel: 'Though the number of the Israelites be like the sand by the sea, only the remnant will be saved. For the Lord will carry out his sentence** [against rebellion] **on earth with speed and finality.' It is just as Isaiah said previously: 'Unless the Lord Almighty had left us descendants, we** [Israel] **would have become like Sodom, we would have been like Gomorrah.** [No one would be saved.]'"

Romans 9:30-33: "**What then shall we say? That the Gentiles, who did not pursue righteousness, have obtained it** [after hearing the gospel], [they have obtained] **a righteousness that is by faith; but the people of Israel, who pursued** [righteousness through obedience to] **the law as the way of righteousness, have not attained their goal.** [Yes, that is what I am saying and] **Why not? Because they** [Israel] **pursued it** [righteousness] **not by faith but as if it were by works. They stumbled over** [the truth, spoken by Jesus] **the stumbling stone. As it is written: 'See, I lay in Zion a stone that causes people to stumble and a rock that makes them fall, and the one who believes in him** [the Rock] **will never be put to shame.'"

Romans Chapter 10

Paul, himself a former Pharisee, explains why Israel failed and why Christians will fail if they follow in the footsteps of the Jews:

Romans 10:1-2: "**Brothers and sisters, my heart's desire and prayer to God for the** [nation of the] **Israelites is that they may be saved. For I can testify about them that they are zealous for God, but their zeal is not based on** [valid] **knowledge.**"

Romans 10:3: "**Since they did not know the righteousness of God and sought to establish their own, they did not submit to God's righteousness** [and this is the crux of the human problem. Abraham and Sarah did not submit to God's righteousness. Jacob and his mother did not submit to God's righteousness. Instead,

---

1   Isaiah 10:22

they each set out to achieve righteousness through works and sinned against God]."

Romans 10:4: "Christ is the culmination of the law [Christ did not sin. Jesus fulfilled all that the law demands. Jesus produced the righteousness which the law declares. The Father sent His Son to achieve this] **so that there may be righteousness** [from God] **for everyone who believes** [in Him]."

"During the days of Jesus' life on earth, he offered up prayers and petitions with fervent cries and tears to the one who could save him from death, and he was heard because of his reverent submission. Son [of God] though he was, he learned obedience from what he suffered and, once made perfect [mature], he became the source of eternal salvation for all who obey him."[1]

Romans 10:5-7: "[Don't be confused. There are two types of righteousness.] **Moses writes this about the** [earthly, manmade] **righteousness that** [comes through obeying the law and] **is** [a righteousness defined] **by the law: 'The person who does these things will live by them.** [This obedience and righteousness is essential for social conduct and order and the happiness of all. If everyone made a sincere effort to exalt the moral code given in the Ten Commandments, life on Earth would be better!]' **But the righteousness that** [I speak of is different. This righteousness is necessary for salvation and it comes only though submission to God's Spirit. This righteousness] **is by faith** [and using the words of Moses,[2] this righteousness] **says: 'Do not say in your heart, "Who will ascend into heaven?"** [to obtain the truth about God's will on these matters]' **(that is,** [Jesus has already come to Earth to reveal the will of God, so there is no need] **to bring Christ down** [again]) **'or** [there is no need to ask] **"Who will descend into the deep?"'** **(that is,** [there is no need] **to bring Christ up from the dead** [to determine God's will, for He has spoken clearly on these matters and He is now risen and sits at the right hand of the Father])."

---

1   Hebrews 5:7-9, italics mine
2   Deuteronomy 30:11-15

Romans 10:8-9: "But what does it [the Scripture] say? 'The word [of God] is near you; it is in your mouth and in your heart,' that is, the message concerning faith that we proclaim [is confirmed by the living Spirit of God. So, given the present persecution of the saints in Rome and the death penalty for serving Christ, you well know]: If you declare with your mouth, 'Jesus is Lord,' and believe in your heart that God raised him from the dead, you will be [condemned to death for saying this, but you also know that you will be] saved [because of your faith in Christ]."

Romans 10:10-13: "For it is with your heart that you believe and are justified, and it is with your mouth that you profess your faith [that Jesus is your king] and [when confronted with death for saying these things, your faith in Christ will not save you from death, but it will save you from the second death. Therefore, as an heir of the righteousness produced by Christ, you] are saved. As Scripture says, 'Anyone who believes in him [Jesus] will never be put to shame.' [So, don't be cowards. Confess to Caesar that "Jesus is Lord." Put your faith in Jesus and leave the consequences with Him.] For [Since the death of Jesus on the cross] there is no difference [in God's sight] between Jew and Gentile—the same Lord is Lord of all [mankind] and [He] richly blesses all who call on him, for, 'Everyone [Jew and Gentile] who calls on the name of the Lord will be saved.'"

Romans 10:14-15: "How, then, can they [the uninformed] call on the one they have not believed in? And how can they believe in the one of whom they have not heard? And how can they hear without someone preaching to them? And how can anyone preach unless they are sent? As it is written[1]: 'How beautiful are the feet of those who bring good news!'"

Romans 10:16-17: "[Don't be discouraged that only a few in Rome have accepted Christ.] But not all the Israelites [have] accepted the good news [either]. For Isaiah says [of rebellious Israel],

---

1   Isaiah 52:7

'Lord, who has believed our message?' Consequently, faith comes from hearing the message, and the message is heard through [preaching and teaching] the word[s] about Christ."

Romans 10:18: "But I ask: Did they [Israel] not hear? Of course they did: [David says in Psalm 19:4 of God's creative works] 'Their voice has gone out into all the earth, their words to the ends of the world.'"

Romans 10:19: "Again I ask: Did Israel not understand? [Israel was given every chance to understand. But, because of defiant rebellion, Israel could not understand.] First, Moses says, 'I will make you envious by those who are not a nation; I will make you angry by a nation that has no understanding.'"

This prediction should have caused every priest and religious teacher in Israel to question his own understanding. Through Moses, the Lord promised to exalt those who are not a nation above the nation of Israel! Also, the Lord promised to exalt a people who have no understanding of God's salvation! How can this be possible and if it is possible, what would cause the Lord to do such a thing? There is only one answer. God warned Israel that if it became rebellious, God would select others as trustees of His gospel. God can rescue sinners without Israel's involvement. Such is the love of God for the people of this Earth and this warning should have been carefully studied by Israel's teachers. They should have known better than to become arrogant and self-righteous, exalting themselves because of Abraham, the patriarchs, the covenants, and all of the other gifts given to Israel by God.

Romans 10:20-21: "And Isaiah[1] boldly says [speaking about Messiah], 'I was found by those who did not seek me; I revealed myself to those who did not ask for me.' But concerning Israel he says, 'All day long I have held out my hands to a disobedient and obstinate people.'"

---

1   Isaiah 65:1-2

Romans Chapter 11

In this chapter, Paul explains that due to Israel's rebellion and unbelief, the nation has been purged and cut off from the gospel of God. Now that the Levitical laws have been abolished,[1] God has created a new body of people comprised of believers (Jews and Gentiles) who received Jesus through faith.[2] Jesus has given spiritual gifts to a new set of trustees (pastors, apostles, teachers) to sanctify this body of people.[3] God's gospel now supports a new body, a self-selecting group of people who follow the Holy Spirit. This new Israel consists of people who *want* to live by faith, people who *want* to grow through sanctification, and people who *want* to glorify the Father and Jesus through good works.[4] This group of people, whose hearts have been circumcised, is the only Israel that matters to God!

Romans 11:1: "[Given Israel's long history of apostasy and rebellion,] **I ask then: Did God reject his people? By no means!** [He has been exceedingly patient with Israel.] **I am an Israelite myself, a descendant of Abraham, from the tribe of Benjamin.** [And I am a beneficiary of God's great mercy on Israel, but Israel has not corporately responded to God in a humble way. In fact, Israel corporately rejected God's gospel spoken by the Word of God,[5] when they hung Jesus on the cross.]"

Romans 11:2-3: "[There remains an Israel of God, but not as a race or a nation.] **God did not reject his people,** [the remnant within Israel] **whom he foreknew. Don't you know what Scripture says in the passage about Elijah—how he appealed to God against Israel: 'Lord, they have killed your prophets and torn down your altars; I am the only one left, and they are trying to kill me'?"

Romans 11:4-6: "And what was God's answer to him? 'I have reserved for myself seven thousand** [a remnant] **who have not**

---

1   Colossians 2
2   Ephesians 2
3   Ephesians 4
4   Ephesians 2:10
5   Revelation 19:13

bowed the knee to Baal.' So too, at the present time there is a **remnant** [a small group of believers in Christ] **chosen by grace** [called like Abraham and through faith they are empowered to carry out God's plans.]. **And if** [they are chosen] **by grace, then it cannot be based on** [their] **works** [that they seek salvation]; **if it were, grace would no longer be grace.**"

Romans 11:7-8: "**What** [am I saying] **then? What the people of Israel sought so earnestly they did not obtain. The** [small] **elect** [group] **among them did** [see how the pieces fit together, and that Jesus is clearly the Son of God. We understand the righteousness that comes through faith in Him*], **but the others** [in Israel] **were hardened** [like Pharaoh], **as it is written**[1]: **'God gave them a spirit of stupor, eyes that could not see and ears that could not hear, to this very day.'** [In other words, God's actions have produced the same result in Israel as in Egypt. The rebellious become defiant, but those who know the Spirit of God choose submission.]"

*Note: Jesus said: *"You are my friends if you do what I command. I no longer call you servants, because a servant does not know his master's business. Instead, I have called you friends, for everything that I learned from my Father I have made known to you. You did not choose me, but I chose you and appointed you so that you might go and bear fruit–fruit that will last–and so that whatever you ask in my name the Father will give you. This is my command: Love each other."*[2]

Romans 11:9-10: "**And David says** [in Psalm 69:22-23 of his own stubborn people]: **'May their table become a snare and a trap, a stumbling block and a retribution for them. May their eyes be darkened so they cannot see, and their backs be bent forever.'**"

Romans 11:11-12: "**Again I ask: Did they** [the nation of Israel] **stumble so as to fall beyond recovery? Not at all! Rather,**

---

1   Isaiah 44:18
2   John 15:14-17, italics mine

[there is a silver lining in this] **because of their transgression, salvation has come to the Gentiles to make Israel envious** [just like Isaiah said]. **But if their** [Israel's] **transgression means riches** [in grace] **for the world, and their loss means riches for the Gentiles, how much greater riches will their full inclusion** [after repentance] **bring!"**

Romans 11:13-14: **"I am talking to you Gentiles** [for a moment]. **Inasmuch as I am the apostle to the Gentiles, I take pride in my ministry** [and speak in glowing terms about what God has done] **in the hope that I may somehow arouse my own people to envy and save some of them."**

Romans 11:15-16: **"For if their rejection** [of God's Truth and His Son, the Messiah,] **brought reconciliation to the world** [Jews and Gentiles], **what will their acceptance** [of Christ] **be but life from the dead?** [We Jews well know that] **If the part of the dough offered as firstfruits is holy, then the whole batch is holy; if the root is holy, so are the branches."**

Romans 11:17-18: **"If some of the branches have been broken off** [because of rebellion], **and you** [Gentiles], **though a wild olive shoot, have been grafted in among the others and now share in the nourishing sap from the olive root, do not consider yourself to be superior to those other branches** [who have been broken off]. **If you do, consider this: You do not support the root, but the root supports you."**

Romans 11:19-21: **"You will say then, 'Branches were broken off so that I could be grafted in.' Granted. But they were broken off because of unbelief, and you** [were grafted in through faith and you can remain as long as you] **stand by faith. Do not be arrogant, but tremble. For if God did not spare the natural branches, he will not spare you either."**

Romans 11:22: **"Consider therefore the kindness and sternness of God: sternness to those who fell** [our forefathers who fell from God's favor because of rebellion], **but kindness to you** [undeserving Gentiles, because you have hearts like Jacob after he repented of his sin, and this kindness from God is endless if you allow Christ to live within you], **provided that you continue in his kindness. Otherwise, you also will be cut off."**

Romans 11:23-24: "And if [individuals in Israel] **they do not persist in unbelief, they will be grafted in, for God is able to graft them in again. After all, if you were cut out of an olive tree that is wild by nature, and contrary to nature were grafted into a cultivated olive tree, how much more readily will these, the natural branches, be grafted into their own olive tree!** [The Jews have a great deal of potential understanding due to their history of the covenants, the law, and the patriarchs. So, they are closer to understanding the many wonderful things of God than Gentiles who know nothing and have heard nothing. Therefore, the Jews could quickly be grafted back into the olive tree if only their hearts were softened and their eyes and ears were opened!]"

Romans 11:25: "[However, and it deeply distresses me,] **I do not want you to be ignorant of this mystery, brothers and sisters, so that you may not be conceited: Israel** [was chosen by God, but she] **has experienced a hardening** [of the heart] **in part until the full number of the Gentiles has come in,** [to the kingdom. The Gentiles will fill up the kingdom of God and it shall come to pass that, 'Israel will be envious of those who are not a nation; and Israel will be angry at a nation that has no understanding.' because God has redefined Israel. Those who believe in Jesus are the heirs of Abraham.]"

[*"So in Christ Jesus you are all children of God through faith, for all of you who were baptized into Christ have clothed yourselves with Christ. There is neither Jew nor Gentile, neither slave nor free, nor is there male and female, for you are all one in Christ Jesus. If you belong to Christ, then you are Abraham's seed [Greek: sperma], and heirs according to the promise."*[1]]

---

1   Galatians 3:26-29, italics mine

Romans 11:26-27: "[Because we know that not all who are descended from the loins of Israel are part of Israel, nor because they are his descendants are they all Abraham's children, it is therefore not the natural children who are God's children. All who are born again are regarded as Abraham's offspring,*] **and in this way all Israel** [everyone who is grafted into the cultivated olive tree] **will be saved. As it is written: 'The deliverer will come from Zion** [New Jerusalem]; **he will turn godlessness away from Jacob.** [He will take away the carnal nature from His people.] **And this is my covenant with them when I take away their sins.**'"**

*Note: *"A person is not a Jew who is one only outwardly, nor is circumcision merely outward and physical. No, a person is a Jew who is one inwardly; and circumcision is circumcision of the heart, by the Spirit, not by the written code. Such a person's praise is not from other people, but from God."[1]*

**Note: *"But God found fault with the people and said: 'The days are coming, declares the Lord, when I will make a new covenant with the people of Israel and with the people of Judah. It will not be like the covenant I made with their ancestors when I took them by the hand to lead them out of Egypt, because they did not remain faithful to my covenant, and I turned away from them, declares the Lord. This is the covenant I will establish with the people of Israel after that time, declares the Lord. I will put my laws in their minds and write them on their hearts. I will be their God, and they will be my people. No longer will they teach their neighbor, or say to one another, "Know the Lord," because they will all know me, from the least of them to the greatest. For I will forgive their wickedness and will remember their sins no more.' By calling this covenant 'new,' he has made the first one obsolete; and what is obsolete and outdated will soon disappear."[2]*

Romans 11:28-29: "As far as the gospel is concerned, they [the nation of Israel] are enemies for your sake; [given my own

1 Romans 2:28-29, italics mine
2 Hebrews 8:8-13, italics mine

suffering at the hands of my people, the hatred of the Jews against Christians is great] **but as far as election is concerned, they** [the remnant of us who came out of Israel] **are loved on account of the patriarchs,** [who honored God with lives of faith and we are loved by God for the same reason] **for God's gifts and his call are irrevocable.** [These can't be changed, but our history is clear: Humble obedience and faith determines who will eternally benefit from His gifts and His calling.]"

Romans 11:30-32: "**Just as you** [Gentiles] **who were at one time disobedient to God have now received mercy as a result of their disobedience, so they too have now become disobedient in order that they too may now receive mercy as a result of God's mercy to you. For God has bound everyone over to disobedience** [we are all prisoners of the carnal heart] **so that he may have mercy on them all.**"

Romans 11:33-34: "**Oh, the depth of the riches of the wisdom and knowledge of God! How unsearchable his judgments, and his paths beyond tracing out! 'Who has known the mind of the Lord? Or who has been his counselor?'**"

Romans 11:35-36: "**'Who has ever given to God, that God should repay them?'** [We owe God everything, yet He gives us everything. What a God!] **For from him and through him and for him are all things. To him be the glory forever! Amen.**"

Romans Chapter 12

Paul pleads for unity, humility, and expressions of genuine love within the church because believers in Christ are brothers, having the same Father:

Romans 12:1: "**Therefore** [in light of what has been said in the previous three chapters], **I urge you, brothers and sisters** [Jews and Gentiles in Christ], **in view of God's mercy** [His favoritism to all of us], **to offer your bodies as a living sacrifice** [totally dedicated to God's service], **holy and pleasing to God—this is your true and proper worship.**"

Romans 12:2: "Do not conform to the pattern of this world [watch out for idolatry which is seductive and enticing – anything more important than God is an idol]**, but be transformed by the renewing of your mind.** [If you feed regularly on movies, TV shows, and magazines, the beauty of God's Word will be dimmed. However, if you regularly shut out the world and prayerfully study the Word of God, the Bible will open up. You will discover many wonderful and interesting treasures about God.] **Then you will be able to test** [and evaluate] **and approve what God's will is—his good, pleasing and perfect will."**

Romans 12:3: "For by the grace given me I say to every one of you: Do not think of yourself more highly than you ought [were it not for your faith in Jesus, you would suffer the same penalty for your sins as those who live in rebellion!]**, but rather think of yourself with sober judgment, in accordance with the faith God has distributed to each of you."**

Romans 12:4-5: "For just as each of us has one body with many members [arms, legs, ears, and eyes]**, and these members do not all have the same function, so in Christ we, though many, form one body, and each member belongs to all the others."**

Romans 12:6-8: "We have different gifts, according to the grace given to each of us. If your gift is prophesying, then prophesy in accordance with your faith; if it is serving, then serve; if it is teaching, then teach; if it is to encourage, then give encouragement; if it is giving, then give generously; if it is to lead, do it diligently; if it is to show mercy, do it cheerfully. [Every member has a gift from God and he can do something for the Lord in proportion to his faith!]**"**

Romans 12:9-12: "Love must be sincere. Hate what is evil; cling to what is good. Be devoted to one another in love. Honor one another above yourselves. Never be lacking in zeal, but keep your spiritual fervor, serving the Lord. Be joyful in hope, patient in affliction, faithful in prayer."

Romans 12:13-15: "Share with the Lord's people who are in need. Practice hospitality. Bless those who persecute you; bless and do not curse. Rejoice with those who rejoice; mourn with those who mourn."

Romans 12:16-18: "Live in harmony with one another. Do not be proud, but be willing to associate with people of low position. Do not be conceited. Do not repay anyone evil for evil. Be careful to do what is right [respectful] in the eyes of everyone [around you]. If it is possible, as far as it depends on you, live at peace with everyone."

Romans 12:19: "[When you suffer injustice,] Do not take revenge, my dear friends, but leave room for God's wrath, for it is written: 'It is mine to avenge; I will repay,' says the Lord."

Romans 12:20-21: "On the contrary: 'If your enemy is hungry, feed him; if he is thirsty, give him something to drink. In doing this, you will heap burning coals on his head.' Do not be overcome by evil, but overcome evil [do not allow evil doers to make you bitter] with good."

Romans Chapter 13

Paul insists that individuals respect and submit to civil authorities:

Romans 13:1: "Let everyone be subject to the governing authorities [government], for there is no authority except that which God has established. The authorities that exist have been established by God. [God designed government to benefit mankind. Of course, it is true that wicked and ruthless men do come to power and there are times when a government fails to benefit its citizens. However, unless or until there is conflict between the authority of man and the authority of God, submit to the governing authorities.]"

Romans 13:2-3: "Consequently, whoever rebels against the authority [of government] is rebelling against what God has instituted, and those who do so will bring judgment [wrath] on themselves. **For rulers** [who are fair and reasonable] **hold no terror for those who do right, but for those who do wrong. Do you want to be free from fear of the one in authority? Then do what is right and you will be commended."**

Romans 13:4: **"For the one in authority is** [accountable to God, his actions will be judged by God, he is] **God's servant for your good. But if you do wrong, be afraid, for rulers do not bear the sword for no reason. They are God's servants, agents of wrath to bring punishment on the wrongdoer.** [If, as a steward of God's authority, a governor shows himself unfit to govern, be patient because God will surely deal with him. Make no mistake about this. God will see to it that every man, whether he is a slave or a king, receives his just and due reward for everything done in the body – whether good or bad.]"

Romans 13:5-6: **"Therefore, it is necessary to submit to the authorities, not only because of possible punishment but also as a matter of conscience. This is also why you pay taxes, for the authorities are God's servants, who give their full time to governing."**

Romans 13:7-8: **"Give to everyone what you owe them: If you owe taxes, pay taxes; if revenue, then revenue; if respect, then respect; if honor, then honor.** [Do everything possible to avoid debt and] **Let no debt remain outstanding, except the continuing debt to love one another, for whoever loves others has fulfilled the law."**

Romans 13:9: **"The** [second tablet had six] **commandments, 'You shall not commit adultery,' 'You shall not murder,' 'You shall not steal,' 'You shall not covet,' and whatever other command there may be, are summed up in this one command: 'Love your neighbor as yourself.'"**

Romans 13:10-12: "[Also, the first tablet had four commandments, "Thou shalt have no other Gods before me," "Thou shalt not bow down and worship any graven images," "Thou shalt not take the Lord's name in vain," and "Remember the Sabbath day to keep it holy" are summed up in this one rule: "Love the Lord thy God with all thy heart, mind, and soul."] **Love does no harm to a neighbor. Therefore love is the fulfillment of the law. And do this, understanding the present time: The hour has already come for you to wake up from your slumber, because our salvation is nearer now than when we first believed. The night is nearly over; the day is almost here. So let us put aside the deeds of darkness and put on the armor of light."**

Romans 13:13-14: **"Let us behave decently, as in the daytime, not in carousing and drunkenness, not in sexual immorality and debauchery, not in dissension and jealousy. Rather, clothe yourselves with the Lord Jesus Christ, and do not** [constantly] **think about how to gratify the desires** [and passions] **of the flesh** [which have to be crucified every day]."

Romans Chapter 14

Paul now urges kindness and compassion for cultural differences with new converts, knowing that in due time, with mature and patient leadership in the church, these matters will resolve:

Romans 14:1: **"Accept the one whose faith is weak** [that is, whose understanding is incomplete and his faith in Christ is new and immature]**, without quarreling** [and condemning him] **over disputable matters.** [Disputable matters are not doctrines. Disputable matters are social and cultural issues. Disputable matters are not to be confused with absolutes declared by God Himself.]"

Romans 14:2: "[For example, I wish to address two problems confronting the church in Rome. Many Gentile converts to Christ are presently eating foods offered to idols. Remember, it was their custom before knowing Christ to seek the blessings of idols with food offerings. They did this long before they ever heard of Jesus. When a Gentile convert realizes an idol is nothing but a stone, what difference does it make if the food has been offered to an idol?

I say this because,] **One person's faith** [in Christ] **allows them to eat anything** [including foods offered to idols], **but another,** [for example, a Jewish convert who has spent a lifetime closely guarding his dietary intake per the Levitical law] **whose faith** [in Christ] **is weak**[, new and immature], **eats only vegetables.** [Be generous and patient with each other in this disputable matter. Culture changes slowly. You may recall when the apostle Peter decided he would not eat and associate with Gentile believers after some Jews arrived in Galatia, I openly rebuked him for it.]"

Romans 14:3: **"The one who** [understands that an idol is nothing but a stone and] **eats everything must not treat with contempt the one who does not, and the one who does not eat everything must not judge the one who does, for God has accepted them** [too]. [I well understand the religious and cultural differences between a Gentile and a Jew – the ways and thoughts of each man are vastly different. Yet, believers in Christ must love one another, support one another, and grant each other the privilege of worshiping God according to the dictates of his conscience.]"

Paul understood that circumstances can produce an honest impasse.[1] However, an impasse should not ruin respect and integrity. When it comes to worship, Paul wrote: **"But everything should be done in a fitting and orderly way."**[2] When there is an honest impasse over Bible truth between believers and unity cannot be sustained because of divergence, there are two remedies: Seek the Lord for clarity and direction with fasting and prayer. If no solution appears within a reasonable and agreeable time frame, rather than arguing to destroy the other person's conclusions, mutually agree there is an honest impasse; then separate with respect and affection for each other. After all, salvation comes through faith (not through knowledge of absolute truth[3]) and each of us must live according to our convictions. Perhaps both groups will flourish and prosper under the Spirit's leadership until the time comes for more truth to

1   Acts 15:36-41
2   1 Corinthians 14:40
3   John 16:13

be revealed. God releases and makes His truth known over time.[1] **"Now [worshiping] the Lord [requires being in] is the Spirit, and where the Spirit of the Lord is, there is freedom."**[2]

Romans 14:4: "[If you hold contempt in your heart for someone whose religious practice is unlike yours, I ask:] **Who are you to judge someone else's servant?** [Every believer in Christ is a servant of God.] **To their own master, [all] servants stand or fall. And they[, whether former Gentiles or Jews,] will stand, for the Lord is able to make them stand."**

Romans 14:5: "[We also have a second disputable problem in the church:] **One person considers one day more sacred than another;** [for example, certain Jewish converts insist on observing Jewish feast days which Israel has celebrated for fourteen hundred years and] **another** [the Gentile] **considers every day alike. Each of them should be fully convinced in their own mind** [as to the will of God on this matter]**."**

Romans 14:6: "**Whoever** [among the Jews] **regards one** [feast] **day as special does so to the Lord. Whoever** [among the Gentiles] **eats meat** [offered to an idol] **does so to the Lord, for they give thanks to God; and whoever abstains** [from eating meat or declaring every day alike] **does so to the Lord and gives thanks to God."**

Romans 14:7-9: "**For none of us lives for ourselves alone, and none of us dies for ourselves alone. If we live, we live for the Lord; and if we die, we die for the Lord. So, whether we live or die, we belong to the Lord. For this very reason, Christ died and returned to life so that he might be the Lord of both the dead and the living."**

Romans 14:10-12: "**You, then, why do you judge** [condemn] **your brother or sister? Or why do you treat them with contempt? For we will all stand before God's judgment seat** [Didn't Jesus say that each of us would be judged with the same measure

---

1   Ephesians 3
2   2 Corinthians 3:17

that we judge others?]. **It is written: " 'As surely as I live,' says the Lord, 'every knee will bow before me; every tongue will acknowledge God.' " So then,** [be mindful of this:] **each of us will give an account of ourselves to God."**

Romans 14:13-14: "Therefore let us stop passing judgment on one another. Instead, make up your mind not to put any stumbling block or obstacle in the way of a brother or sister. I am convinced, being fully persuaded in the Lord Jesus [for several years], **that nothing** [offered to idols] **is unclean in itself. But if anyone regards something as unclean**[, he has a conviction], **then for that person it is unclean."**

Romans 14:15-18: "If your brother or sister is distressed because of what you eat, you are no longer acting in love [if you continue to distress him]. **Do not by your eating destroy someone for whom Christ died. Therefore** [, on the other hand,] **do not let what you know is good be spoken of as evil.** [Do not go along without speaking up on what is good. If possible, work out your differences with Scripture. If this is not possible, then mutually agree on an honest impasse. Show respect for all who love the Lord, even though they may have opposing views about foods offered to idols and the observance of feast days.] **For the kingdom of God is not a matter of eating and drinking, but of righteousness, peace and joy in the Holy Spirit, because anyone who serves Christ in this way is pleasing to God and receives human approval."**

Romans 14:19-21: "Let us therefore make every effort to do what leads to peace and to mutual edification. Do not destroy the work of God for the sake of food. All food [offered to idols] **is clean** [if God has first declared it to be clean], **but it is wrong for a person to eat anything that causes someone else to stumble. It is better not to eat meat or drink wine or to do anything else that will cause your brother or sister to fall."**

Romans 14:22-23: "So whatever you believe about these things keep between yourself and God [do not create open conflict on these disputable matters]. **Blessed is the one who does not condemn himself by what he approves. But whoever has doubts is** [already] **condemned if they eat** [something their conscience condemns], **because their eating is not from faith** [it is violating their own conscience]; **and everything that does not come from faith is sin**[, therefore, obey the conviction which the Holy Spirit brings. He leads us through knowledge and faith into the fullness of Christ]**."**

Romans Chapter 15

Paul appeals for Christian tolerance, not in the sense of ignoring or going along with evil,[1] but graciously tolerating the cultural and religious views of those who show genuine fruit of the Spirit:

Romans 15:1-2: "We who are strong ought to bear [patiently] **with the failings of the weak and not to please ourselves.** [Yes, you may be in the right, but what good is your position on a disputable matter if it causes your brother to stumble? Outside moral issues,] **Each of us should please our neighbors for their good, to build them up."**

[*"I [Paul] wrote to you [the church in Corinth] in my letter not to associate with sexually immoral people–not at all meaning the people of this world who are immoral, or the greedy and swindlers, or idolaters. In that case you would have to leave this world. But now I am writing to you that you must not associate with anyone who claims to be a brother or sister but is sexually immoral or greedy, an idolater or slanderer, a drunkard or swindler. Do not even eat with such people. What business is it of mine to judge those outside the church? Are you not to judge those inside? God will judge those outside. 'Expel the wicked person from among you.'"*[2]]

Romans 15:3-4: "For even Christ did not please himself but, as it is written: 'The insults of those who insult you have fallen on me.' For everything that was written in the past was written to teach

---

1   1 Corinthians 5:1-11; Revelation 2:20
2   1 Corinthians 5:9-13, italics mine

us, so that through the endurance taught in the Scriptures and the encouragement they provide we might have hope."

Romans 15:5-7: "May the God who gives endurance and encouragement give you the same attitude of mind toward each other that Christ Jesus had, so that with one mind and one voice you may glorify the God and Father of our Lord Jesus Christ. Accept one another, then, just as Christ accepted you, in order to bring praise to God."

Romans 15:8-9: "For I tell you that Christ has become a servant of the Jews on behalf of God's truth, so that the promises made to the patriarchs might be confirmed and, moreover, that the Gentiles might glorify God for his mercy. As it is written: 'Therefore I will praise you among the Gentiles; I will sing the praises of your name.'"

Romans 15:10-13: "Again, it says, 'Rejoice, you Gentiles, with his people.' And again, 'Praise the Lord, all you Gentiles; let all the peoples extol him.' And again, Isaiah says, 'The Root of Jesse will spring up, one who will arise to rule over the nations; in him the Gentiles will hope.' May the God of hope fill you with all joy and peace as you trust in him, so that you may overflow with hope by the power of the Holy Spirit."

Romans 15:14-16: "I myself am convinced, my brothers and sisters, that you yourselves are full of goodness, filled with knowledge and competent to instruct one another. Yet I have written you quite boldly on some points to remind you of them again, because of the grace God gave me to be a minister of Christ Jesus to the Gentiles. He gave me the priestly duty of proclaiming the gospel of God [without regard to our carnal nature], so that the Gentiles might become an offering acceptable to God, sanctified by the Holy Spirit."

Romans 15:17-19: "Therefore I glory in Christ Jesus in my service to God. I will not venture to speak of anything except what Christ has accomplished through me in leading the

Gentiles to obey God by what I have said and done—by the power of signs and wonders, through the power of the Spirit of God. So from Jerusalem all the way around to Illyricum, I have fully proclaimed the gospel of Christ."

Romans 15:20-22: "It has always been my ambition to preach the gospel where Christ was not known, so that I would not be building on someone else's foundation. Rather, as it is written: 'Those who were not told about him will see [Jesus], and those who have not heard will understand [His salvation]." This is why I have often been hindered from coming to you.'

Romans 15:23-24: "But now that there is no more place for me to work in these regions, and since I have been longing for many years to visit you, I plan to do so when I go to Spain. I hope to see you while passing through and to have you assist me on my journey there, after I have enjoyed your company for a while."

Romans 15:25-27: "Now, however, I am on my way to Jerusalem in the service of the Lord's people there. For Macedonia and Achaia were pleased to make a contribution for the poor among the Lord's people in Jerusalem. They were pleased to do it, and indeed they owe it to them. For if the Gentiles have shared in the Jews' spiritual blessings, they owe it to the Jews [Jewish converts who have lost everything for following Jesus] to share with them their material blessings."

Romans 15:28-33: "So after I have completed this task and have made sure that they have received this contribution, I will go to Spain and visit you on the way. I know that when I come to you, I will come in the full measure of the blessing of Christ. I urge you, brothers and sisters, by our Lord Jesus Christ and by the love of the Spirit, to join me in my struggle by praying to God for me. Pray that I may be kept safe from the unbelievers in Judea [my own race] and that the contribution I take to Jerusalem may be favorably received by the Lord's people there, so that I may come to you with joy, by God's will, and in your company be refreshed. The God of peace be with you all. Amen."

Romans Chapter 16

Paul adds a postscript to his letter; he warmly greets some of his friends and believers in Rome:

Romans 16:1-2: "I commend to you our sister Phoebe, a deacon of the church in Cenchreae. I ask you to receive her in the Lord in a way worthy of his people and to give her any help she may need from you, for she has been the benefactor of many people, including me."

Romans 16:3-5: "Greet Priscilla and Aquila, my co-workers in Christ Jesus. They risked their lives for me. Not only I but all the churches of the Gentiles are grateful to them. Greet also the church that meets at their house. Greet my dear friend Epenetus, who was the first convert to Christ in the province of Asia."

Romans 16:6-10: "Greet Mary, who worked very hard for you. Greet Andronicus and Junia, my fellow Jews who have been in prison with me. They are outstanding among the apostles, and they were in Christ before I was. Greet Ampliatus, my dear friend in the Lord. Greet Urbanus, our co-worker in Christ, and my dear friend Stachys. Greet Apelles, whose fidelity to Christ has stood the test. Greet those who belong to the household of Aristobulus."

Romans 16:11-13: "Greet Herodion, my fellow Jew. Greet those in the household of Narcissus who are in the Lord. Greet Tryphena and Tryphosa, those women who work hard in the Lord. Greet my dear friend Persis, another woman who has worked very hard in the Lord. Greet Rufus, chosen in the Lord, and his mother, who has been a mother to me, too."

Romans 16:14-16: "Greet Asyncritus, Phlegon, Hermes, Patrobas, Hermas and the other brothers and sisters with them. Greet Philologus, Julia, Nereus and his sister, and Olympas and all the Lord's people who are with them. Greet one another with a holy kiss. All the churches of Christ send greetings."

Romans 16:17-18: "I urge you, brothers and sisters, to watch out for those who cause divisions and put obstacles in your way that are contrary to the teaching you have learned. Keep away from them. For such people are not serving our Lord Christ, but their own appetites. By smooth talk and flattery they deceive the minds of naive people."

Romans 16:19-20: "Everyone has heard about your obedience, so I rejoice because of you; but I want you to be wise about what is good, and innocent about what is evil. The God of peace will soon crush Satan under your feet. The grace of our Lord Jesus be with you."

Romans 16:21-23: "Timothy, my co-worker, sends his greetings to you, as do Lucius, Jason and Sosipater, my fellow Jews. I, Tertius, who wrote down this letter, greet you in the Lord. Gaius, whose hospitality I and the whole church here enjoy, sends you his greetings. Erastus, who is the city's director of public works, and our brother Quartus send you their greetings."

Romans 16:24: "[May the grace of our Lord Jesus Christ be with all of you. Amen.][1]"

Romans 16:25-27: "Now to him who is able to establish you in accordance with my gospel, the message I proclaim about Jesus Christ, in keeping with the revelation of the mystery hidden for long ages past, but now revealed and made known through the prophetic writings by the command of the eternal God, so that all the Gentiles might come to the obedience that comes from faith—to the only wise God be glory forever through Jesus Christ! Amen"

1   Included in some manuscripts.

About the Author

Larry Wilson became a born-again Christian after returning from a tour of duty in Vietnam. His understanding of the gospel, the plan of salvation, and the atonement of Jesus Christ thrilled his soul his entire life. He spent over 40 years intensely studying the prophecies of Daniel and Revelation. In 1988, he published his first book and later authored many other books. Over one million of his books are in circulation throughout the world.

About the Organization

Wake Up America Seminars (WUAS) is both a non-profit and a non-denominational organization. With God's blessings and the generosity of many people, WUAS has distributed millions of pamphlets, books and tapes around the world since it began in 1988. WUAS is not a church and is not affiliated or sponsored by any religious organization. It promotes the primacy of salvation through faith in Jesus Christ, His imminent return, and is doing its best to encourage people with the good news of the gospel.

We encourage you to visit our website for further study. Most of the study materials that Larry Wilson has produced during his forty years of ministry are available for free at *wake-up.org.*

Watch free videos at *wake-up.org/video-series-list* or *youtube. com/wuaseminars*

If you have comments about this book or questions, please send them to us at the email or physical address below.

Wake Up America Seminars, Inc.
P.O. Box 273
Bellbrook, OH 45305
wake-up.org
email: *wuaseminars@gmail.com*